Self-Discipline Mastery

Develop Navy Seal Mental Toughness, Unbreakable Grit, a Spartan Mindset, Build Good Habits, and Increase Your Productivity

Self-Discipline Mastery

PUBLISHED BY: James W. Williams

© **Copyright 2020 - All rights reserved.**

The content contained within this book may not be reproduced, duplicated or transmitted without direct written permission from the author or the publisher.

Under no circumstances will any blame or legal responsibility be held against the publisher, or author, for any damages, reparation, or monetary loss due to the information contained within this book. Either directly or indirectly.

Legal Notice:

This book is copyright protected. This book is only for personal use. You cannot amend, distribute, sell, use, quote or paraphrase any part, or the content within this book, without the consent of the author or publisher.

Disclaimer Notice:

Please note the information contained within this document is for educational and entertainment purposes only. All effort has been executed to present accurate, up to date, and reliable, complete information. No warranties of any kind are declared or implied. Readers acknowledge that the author is not engaging in the rendering of legal, financial, medical or professional advice. The content within this book has been derived from various sources.

Self-Discipline Mastery

Please consult a licensed professional before attempting any techniques outlined in this book.

By reading this document, the reader agrees that under no circumstances is the author responsible for any losses, direct or indirect, which are incurred as a result of the use of information contained within this document, including, but not limited to, — errors, omissions, or inaccuracies

James W. Williams

Table of Contents

Your Free Gift 1

Introduction 3

Chapter 1: The Science of Self-Discipline, Motivation, and Willpower 6

   Habits and Willpower: Engines behind Change and Progress 6

      The Energy/Strength Model 7

      Can Self-Discipline Be Enhanced? 8

Chapter 2: Shifting Your Mindset 18

   What Is a Mindset? 19

   Changing Your Mindset 21

      1. Accept your mistakes and learn lessons from them 21

      2. Set small goals 22

      3. Learn to find inspiration from any source 24

      4. Practice meditation 25

      5. Find three positive changes each day 26

      6. Accept these three truths 27

Chapter 3: Building Good Habits and Breaking Bad Ones 29

   The Little Habits That Make Up Your Day 31

   Ivan Pavlov and Classical Conditioning 32

The Three-Step Loop in Habit Formation 35

How The Three-Step Loop Works 38

Big Actions vs. Small Specific Actions 41

Easy and Simple Actions vs. Complex Actions 42

Physical Actions vs. Mental or Emotional States/Decisions 43

Using Visual and Auditory Cues 46

Building Habits That Stick 46

   Tactic #1: Mini-Goals and Micro Quotas 47

   Tactic #2: Use Behavior Chains 49

   Tactic #3: Visualize Your Goal the Right Way 50

How to Quit Bad Habits 57

Top 10 Bad Habits 57

Breaking Bad Habits 59

   Identify the Reward 59

   Punishment vs. Reward Removal 60

   Replacing the Bad Habit 61

   Tell a Friend 63

   Small and Big Rewards 64

   Is It a Habit or Is It an Addiction? 65

How to Practice Delayed Gratification and How to Overcome Temptations 68

What is Delayed Gratification? 68

It All Began with a Marshmallow 70

Practical Benefits of Delayed Gratification 73

What Determines Your Ability to Practice Delayed Gratification 74

How to Get Better at Delayed Gratification and Overcoming Temptations 76

    Start Small.. 76

    Find Out What is Holding You Back......................... 77

    Expect to Fail and Create a Plan When You Fail 78

    Focus on the Process Not the Performance 80

Sturgeon's Law and the Pareto Principle 82

Essential Habit #1 – How to Build and Stick to a Workout Plan 85

    Keep It Short and Consistent 86

    Break Things Up 86

    Be Accountable 87

    Add Variety 87

    Have Fun 88

Essential Habit #2 – Maintain a Healthy Diet ... 89

    Start with Realistic Expectations 90

    Clean Up Your Pantry/Fridge 90

    Find Out What Really Motivates You 92

    Skip the All or Nothing Mindset 93

    Change Your Diet and Exercise Plan at the Same Time.. 93

- Have a Healthy Snack in Your Pocket Always 94
- Plan Ahead When You Go Out or Travel 95
- Start Your Day with a High Protein Breakfast 96
- Remember That It Takes Time to Change Your Eating Habits 96

Essential Habit #3 – Sleep/Wake Up Early 98

- Signs That You May Be Sleep-Deprived 99
- Why Is It Difficult to Wake Up in the Morning 100
- How to Wake Up Early in the Morning 100
  - Improve Bedtime Routines 101
  - Move Your Alarm Further Away 102
  - Exercise Regularly 103
  - Get Some More Sunlight 103
- When All Else Fails 104

Essential Habit #4 – Work Smart: Eat the Frog 106

- Where Did That Phrase Come From? 106
- Which is Your Biggest Frog? 107
- The Rationale behind the Frog-Eating Habit 108
  - Too Many Meetings 109
  - Dive! Dive! Dive! 109
  - No Shortcuts 110

Essential Habit #5 – Mindfulness 111

- What is Mindfulness? 111

How Can You Benefit from a Mindfulness Habit? 113

Benefit #1: Prevents Overthinking and Anxiety 113

Benefit #2: Improves Performance, Concentration, and Memory 114

Benefit #3: Cognitive Flexibility 115

Benefit #4: Alleviates Stress 115

Benefit #5: Improves Sleep 116

How to Practice Mindfulness Now 117

Step #1: Allocate a space and choose a time for mindfulness practice 118

Step #2: Focus and choose to do so despite distractions and challenges 120

Step #3: Allow yourself that time to do nothing ... 120

Step #4: Try not to look at the clock 121

Step #5: Pay attention but don't judge and let it all pass 121

Step #6: Acknowledge your self-judgments and self-doubt 122

Step #7: Return to the Present 123

Mindfulness Meditation Sample: Body Scan 124

Chapter 4: More Actionable Tips to Build Self-Discipline 129

That One Simple Trick That Will Boost Your Motivation to Do Anything 130

Beating the Traditional Model for Motivation 131

Working with the Science behind Motivation 133

That One Simple Trick 134

Move Towards Discomfort – How Discomfort Builds Character 136

    Discomfort, Pain, and Chaos Builds Character 136

    A Paradigm Shift 138

Intermittent Fasting 138

    Intermittent Fasting: What It Is 140

    Methods of Intermittent Fasting 141

    How to Stick to an Intermittent Fasting Regimen 143

Cold Showers 145

    What Are Cold Showers? 145

    Benefits of Cold Showers Proven by Science 146

    It's Not a Cure-All 147

    How to Make the Cold Shower a Habit 148

100 Days of Rejection Therapy 149

    Benefits of Rejection Therapy 150

Building Routines 152

    How a Routine Will Make You More Disciplined . 153

    Downsides That You Should Know About 155

    How to Create a Healthy Mindful Routine 156

Chapter 5: Dealing with Burnout the Smart Way 160

What is a Work Burnout Exactly? 161

Three Types of Burnout 162

Different Modes of Measuring Exhaustion and Burnout 164

A Short History about the Concept of a Burnout 166

Who Can Get Affected by Burnouts 167

Be Aware of the Burnout Signs: Some Important Q&A 169

    List of Psychological Symptoms You May Experience 171

    List of Physical Symptoms You May Experience ... 172

    Key Symptoms That You Should Look Out For 173

Causes of Burnouts 176

Burnout Prevention 179

    Increase Self-Efficacy 179

Chapter 6 – Discipline Tactics of Navy SEALs and the Spartans 185

Success = Discipline 185

Military Secrets 186

    Don't Quit 186

    Always Make Every Goal and Objective a Serious Thing 187

    Wake Up Early and Win the Morning 187

    Pay Attention to Every Lesson That You Learn 189

    Exercise 189

    Embrace the Suck 190

Mastering the Art of Simplicity 191
You're Never Really Alone 195
You Need to Challenge Yourself Constantly 198

Conclusion **201**
Thank you! **202**
Resource Page **203**

Your Free Gift

As a way of saying thanks for your purchase, I wanted to offer you a free bonus E-book called **Bulletproof Confidence** exclusive to the readers of this book.

To get instant access just go to:

https://theartofmastery.com/confidence/

Inside the book, you will discover:
- What is shyness & social anxiety, and the psychology behind it
- Simple yet powerful strategies for overcoming social anxiety

- Breakdown of the traits of what makes a confident person
- Traits you must DESTROY if you want to become confident
- Easy techniques you can implement TODAY to keep the conversation flowing
- Confidence checklist to ensure you're on the right path of self-development

Introduction

Would you listen to a businessman and author who has failed a hundred times and has failed miserably at that? Should you?

Well, you should.

You see, there is wisdom in listening to mistakes and failure, and you learn vicariously through the experience of others. By doing that, you get to improve a lot faster than I ever did.

Imagine setting up business after business only to see them fail. Imagine lacking the knowledge, making the mistakes, and then relapsing into a muck of failure complete with self-loathing and total lack of discipline.

What does it take to get over that?

The answer for me was my self-discipline, grit, and mental toughness that I developed over the years. And in this book, I outline not just the mistakes I made but how I bounced back from them using the lessons I've learned. But I didn't make that transformation on my own.

I learned from countless mentors and coaches so that I could go back into my little mouse wheel and strive once again for success. A lot of them were from countless hours of reading and researching the most disciplined and successful people in history.

It took a lot of practice and perseverance to develop a shift in mindset. I drew from all of that experience when I wrote this book. It is a collection of thoughts, ideas, practices, personal experience, and coaching from some of the most disciplined people on earth.

Was it easy to try and regain self-control and muster enough willpower?

It was never *easy*. But the journey back to self-mastery and the friendships that I made along the way have made it all worthwhile. I have learned to apply mental fortitude and self-discipline in business, family life, and now in writing as well.

This book is my way of giving back to everyone who may have lost their way too—just like me. The lessons and practices here from mental toughness to meditation have helped me accomplish things that I never imagined I could.

If you immerse yourself in the principles that I have learned and outlined in this book, you will also learn how to put everything on the line and strive for the goal like there's nothing left to lose.

May the information here be a powerful guide for you as it was for me.

Chapter 1: The Science of Self-Discipline, Motivation, and Willpower

"Discipline is the bridge between goals and accomplishments."

(Jim Rohn)

Do you want to enhance your self-discipline, increase your willpower, and improve self-motivation? One of the secrets to achieving all of that is to develop habits and willpower. Experts say that these are two important keys to every accomplishment that has been measured in the modern world.

Habits and Willpower: Engines behind Change and Progress

Willpower is the thing that drives us to save for our future. Habits, on the other hand, establish patterns that lead to success and progress. These principles drive us to keep on working even if we don't want to or when we don't feel like it.

It is our willpower that makes us say no to that cigarette, no to that whiskey, and no to that extra helping of cake. It is willpower that makes us hop on that treadmill, report to the gym, and be patient with a wayward child.

When willpower fails, our self-discipline fails. Where willpower pushes us to go on the right path, our actions become habits, and our habits determine what we ultimately can achieve.

The Energy/Strength Model

Willpower, habits, self-discipline, and motivation are all interrelated. They are also subjects that have been studied extensively [1] by psychiatrists and other experts as well. When it comes to self-control and self-discipline, one of the reigning theories is called the energy model, or strength model [2].

According to this model, the brain is viewed as something akin to a muscle. And just like any muscle, it is seen as one that also has a limited amount of strength. It has limits just like any other part of the body.

Can this energy source of the brain be depleted? Yes, it can be depleted via mental exertion. That means no one is disciplined all the time. Every human being will act without discipline every once in a while.

Can Self-Discipline Be Enhanced?

Again, following the energy model, the answer to the question of whether self-discipline can be improved or not, the answer is yes, you can build self-discipline and self-control [3]. Of course, not everyone agrees with the energy model. However, everyone agrees that one can increase in self-discipline with practice.

The next question now is, how do you master, or at least improve, self-discipline? Here are a few tips that you can start with. We will go over more ideas and strategies later in this book.

Forgive Yourself

Sometimes people lose motivation for change simply because they beat themselves up for past mistakes and foibles. Remember that even with all your best intentions and your best effort, you will at one time or another fall short.

All well-laid plans will fail at some time. Remember that it doesn't happen only to you—it happens to everyone. If you fail, learn to acknowledge that fact. Pick yourself up and move on.

One of the ways to learn how to acknowledge past faults and get over them is to practice mindfulness. We will go over mindfulness and how you can use it to overcome shame and guilt due to past mistakes in chapter 3 of this book.

For now, understand that you will have to learn to forgive yourself before you can move on to better things. Self-discipline also involves forgiveness of oneself.

Pay Yourself First

Paying yourself first before anyone or anything else is a powerful motivator. If you don't, then you will get the impression that all your hard work just passes by without you noticing. Paying and rewarding yourself first gives you something to be excited about.

It doesn't have to be a big reward. It can be as simple as a dessert that you have always wanted. It can be a little quiet time that you promised yourself a long time ago. Sometimes you can reward yourself by spending time with friends and family.

Anticipating a reward can be a powerful tool to motivate you to stay the course. It can be something that you can use to obsess about the process that you are going through. You are not only going to think about the changes that you are making, but you've also got the reward in mind as well.

Make a Backup Plan and Plan for the Worst

Again, we mentioned earlier that everyone fails, right? So what do you do? You create a backup plan. A technique that you can use to boost your willpower during trying times is what psychiatric experts call *implementation intention* [4].

In simple terms, it is a plan that you can implement whenever you are faced with an anticipated difficult situation. It is a backup plan that you have prepared for the worst-case scenarios that you can imagine.

For example, you want to lose weight, and you are following a low-carb diet plan. What's a possible worst-case scenario? Here's one—you went out to have dinner with your friends. Unfortunately, all the food that's on the menu is unhealthy and rich in carbohydrates.

What do you do?

Before you dive into that scrumptious chocolate cake, you should have made your preparations for such an occasion beforehand. You pack a favorite low-carb snack, and while having the meal with your friends, you just order a nice low-carb drink—worst case, it will only be water, but tea minus the sugar or sweeteners should be fine as well.

While in the diner or restaurant (or wherever it is you went to eat) you planned to focus on having a great conversation with your friends. And that is how you planned to overcome the temptation to break your low-carb diet.

Realign Your Beliefs

Studies [5] show that the amount of willpower that you have is deeply rooted in your personal beliefs. If you believe that you have very little control and a limited amount of willpower, then that will be your truth even though you can summon more, but you just weren't aware of it.

The secret, of course, is to change your inner conceptions. Change how you see yourself, and your true potential and worth will eventually increase. Think along the lines of Napoleon Hill's famous statement:

> *"Whatever the mind can conceive and believe, it can achieve."*

Your beliefs have a huge impact on your behavior, according to a 2007 study published in the *Journal of Applied Social Psychology*. If you want to increase mental toughness, self-discipline, and have unbreakable grit, you need to realign your negative beliefs and limiting beliefs and form positive and empowering beliefs.

Here are a few tips on how you can do that:

1. Identify Your Feelings

How do you feel about a certain task or a goal? For instance, do you feel confident that you can make a million dollars in the next three years? How do you feel about losing weight and trimming down to two clothing sizes in the next six months?

The first step is to identify these negative feelings. These feelings contribute to limiting beliefs, and you must identify them first before you can change the negative belief associated with that feeling.

2. Accept Your Feelings

You can't deny your feelings. You experience them, and therefore they are evident. However, you should also realize this truth—your feelings are not permanent. You can feel sad one moment but then feel happy, the total opposite, a few minutes later.

By that same token, you may feel that you can't hit this month's sales quota. However, that feeling can also change to you can—especially after closing your next sale. Then you will begin to see the possibilities and change how you feel about yourself and your capabilities.

3. <u>Replacing Old Realities with New Ones</u>

As your feelings change, you change your perceptions. You experience what Stephen Covey calls a *paradigm shift*. Paradigm shifts don't have to be huge and world-changing. They can be small but significant, like saying no to that extra helping in a buffet.

When you do that, you begin to understand that you already have the capacity to lose weight and stick to a diet plan. When you close the next sale, you begin to see that this is something that you can do.

You change your paradigm, you change your reality. In effect, you change how you see yourself, and you change how you see the world. Your positive experiences are not the only source of positive or reinforcing beliefs—you can use the experiences of others and concepts that have been taught or shared with you as the basis and evidence for positive feelings and beliefs.

4. **Repeat the New Truths That You Have Discovered**

Where you used to tell yourself that you can't do it, tell yourself that you can. Use the evidence that you drew upon in step number three to reinforce your new beliefs. You need to repeat and reinforce these beliefs, especially when you experience setbacks and failures.

It will take some time, but you will realize that every failure is but a proverbial stepping stone toward success. Failure is part of the process. Remind yourself of your new truths.

By realigning your beliefs, you slowly feed your self-confidence. Your improved self-confidence improves your mindset and contributes to your level of mental toughness. You begin to understand that despite your failures, you are an achiever.

Eat Often and Eat Healthy

Unless you intend to practice intermittent fasting, it should be a priority to eat healthy and to eat often. Research [6] suggests that the resolve and willpower of people go down when their blood sugar levels go down.

Do you notice that your ability to focus and concentrate is greatly diminished when your stomach is growling? You need to fuel up if you want to increase your resolve to do what is needed, but remember to eat healthy always.

Work on Small and Simple New Habits

Complex habits will be harder to develop. The solution is to choose simple and easy habits and build on them [7]. For example, do you find that working out in the gym for two hours is just way too much?

You can resolve that by reducing your workout time to 15 to 30 minutes. Another alternative is to work out at home. If you have trouble getting enough sleep, don't aim for the full six to eight hours at first. Start by sleeping 15 minutes earlier than usual. You can increase the number of minutes until you get to the full amount of sleep you wanted to get.

By working on small and achievable habits, they eventually add up to bigger habits. Smaller habits require smaller disciplined steps that are easier to achieve. Small achievements help to reinforce your self-confidence.

In the next chapter, we will go over what mindset is and how you can shift your mindset to gain more self-discipline.

Chapter 2: Shifting Your Mindset

"Once your mindset changes, everything on the outside will change along with it."

(Steve Maraboli)

A standard textbook definition of the word *mindset* goes something like this: it is an established set of thoughts and attitudes that have been selected and held by someone. In psychology, a person's mindset is that belief or set of beliefs that guide the way people handle situations [8].

That last definition above was by Dr. Gary Klein. He further explains that our mindsets help us do things and determine things. For instance, with our current mindset, we judge whether we are looking at an opportunity or not.

Our mindsets can be self-defeating, but they can also be progressive and beneficial. Self-discipline is, first and foremost, strongly tied to one's mindset. Your attitude toward something will determine whether you will pursue a disciplined approach about it or not.

If you want to be more disciplined and have more self-control, then you need to change your mindset.

What Is a Mindset?

Professor Carol Dweck of Stanford University popularized the idea of mindsets in 2006. She contrasted people's beliefs about the source of their abilities. She observed that when people have a fixed mindset that they have innate abilities.

This can be a dangerous situation because when they encounter failure, their mindset is challenged, and so is their self-esteem, so their self-confidence is also called into question. Such an experience can make people doubt their true potential.

Dweck, on the other hand, pointed out that there is a fixed mindset and a growth mindset. A growth mindset is very different. It is a point of view that you are adept at improving your capabilities. It is the attitude that accepts mistakes and expects continuous growth.

With that type of mindset, failure is nothing more than an indication of what people need to work on. There are other key differences that she pointed out in her research.

For instance, people with a fixed mindset tended to go out and prove themselves to others. When someone would suggest that they have made a mistake, they would take a defensive stance. They also tend to measure themselves using their failures as the decisive factors.

People with a growth mindset tend to be more resilient. They don't mind making mistakes, and they are often better at persevering. Thus, they are more motivated and usually are more of a hard worker.

Note that these aren't the only types of mindsets. There are others. We just used these two to point out the contrasting facets of different mindsets.

Now, as you can see, some mindsets can be beneficial, and some mindsets can be detrimental. If you want to progress, be more disciplined, and become more successful, then you need to experience a shift in mindset.

Changing Your Mindset

Here are the steps necessary to trigger a shift in one's mindset:

1. Accept your mistakes and learn lessons from them

A truly successful person can readily make a list of his failures. They can be an open book and tell you right then and there how and where they failed and made mistakes. They can also tell you exactly what lessons they learned from those failures.

If you want to learn how to shift your mindset to a more progressive and growth-centered one, then one of the first things you should learn to do is to accept that you have made mistakes along the way.

In my efforts at growing businesses, I remember making all sorts of mistakes from hiring too many personnel, spending too little on advertising, not paying attention to order flows, not listening to customers, and many others.

From the many setbacks that I experienced, I learned a lot of valuable lessons. Mistakes can be a powerful teacher. An entrepreneur that is open about blunders is better able to cope with difficulties because they have growth as their primary centers.

I have learned how to get up from the failure, analyze where I got it wrong, and then lead everyone to better opportunities. The better you are at handling losses, the better you will be at shifting mindsets.

2. Set small goals

Sometimes we get so busy doing the daily grind that we lose sight of our goals. At times we focus too much on the large long-term goal that we fail to measure our progress. We sometimes are fooled into thinking that we aren't progressing and that we aren't capable of a mindset shift.

Take the time to sit down and break down your large long-term goal into smaller short-term goals. Set these goals on a timeline and try to achieve them one at a time. When you accomplish a small goal or mini-goal, go out and celebrate—not too lavish, but enough to remind you that you are already progressing towards that much-awaited mindset shift.

For instance, if you want to shift from the "I am a bad salesman" mindset to the "I'm the greatest salesman" mindset, you don't have to wait until you have made a million-dollar sale.

You can set mini-goals along the way and use them as stepping stones to reach your overall goal. Here are some achievable mini-goals that you can set on the way to becoming the best salesman that you can be:

- Contact the first 100 people and get rejected 100 times
- Find your first three leads
- Get your first seven leads
- Sign up your first 21 people
- Get rejected 200 times
- Convert your first customer from your accumulated leads
- Convert five more leads into customers
- Make 30 new customers
- Get your first three repeat orders
- Get your next ten repeat orders

- Get your first 100 leads/200 leads/300 leads
- Reach up to 100 customers
- Hit your first $1,000 sale (you can set the figure that you want)
- Make your first $3,000 sale
- Achieve $5,000 in sales in one month (again, the figures are all up to you)

You set the mini-goals that you would like to achieve. If you are a writer, then set mini-goals like writing a 300-word article each day, your first newsletter, completing one chapter in your new book each month, or maybe writing a blog post each week. If you want to be more disciplined when it comes to working out, then you can start by committing to go jogging for five minutes each day. You can then slowly work that up to ten minutes two weeks later, and then up to fifteen minutes the following month.

3. Learn to find inspiration from any source

No one has a monopoly on genius. Take some time each day to find inspiration even in the small things. It can come from your employees, your next-door neighbor, and even that irritating landlord.

Read blogs, watch motivational videos, read self-help books, attend webinars, listen to podcasts, and take part in master classes. To truly gain a shift in mindset, you should immerse yourself in the views of others and learn to pick up golden nuggets of wisdom that can be useful to you.

Your point of view won't change unless you expose your mind to insights and ideas from other people. Your mindset won't shift unless it has something to shift into, ergo finding ideas and inspiration from coaches, professors, and other experts in their respective fields.

4. Practice meditation

In the next chapter, we will cover mindfulness and mindfulness meditation. Meditation is a great way to flex your mental muscles, so to speak. Think of meditation as a tool that you can use to calm your mind and stretch your mental faculties to new limits.

If you want to try meditation for at least ten minutes a day, then I recommend that you download the Headspace app on your phone. The first ten days are free, and it will give you a good introduction to meditation. You can also read more about mindfulness in the next chapter.

5. Find three positive changes each day

You think you're not growing or progressing? You might be surprised to find that you are actually going through a lot of positive changes each day, and you just never knew it.

These changes can be ones that are happening (or have happened) to you personally or to someone you know or someone you're associated with. It can be changes that happen in your home.

The goal is to train your mind to see the bright side of things. One day you will notice that even the negative and bad events in your life were actually for your benefit.

6. Accept these three truths

This one is from an executive friend of mine who is quite successful. She says there are three truths you should learn to accept in order to help you embrace a shift in your mindset.

The three truths that she was referring to are:

1. Life is short (so let things slide and don't worry or fuss about things that may offend you)
2. Time is precious (spend it wisely and delegate as much as you can)
3. Your ego will always need to be tamed (it will take time to learn humility)

Remember that change is inevitable. In fact, in many instances, change is good. Your mindset is an ever-growing thing. Embracing that growth is equivalent to embracing your progression.

Why Changing Your Mindset Builds Self-Discipline

Your mindset is your own set of thoughts, beliefs, and attitudes that you have selected for yourself. If you want more self-discipline, you need to change your attitudes and point of view.

Self-Discipline Mastery

If you used to think that work is something unpleasant, then you should change your mindset and start seeing your work as a means of getting something better in your life.

Changing your mindset changes your attitudes towards losing weight. By seeing weight loss as something achievable, then you gain enough grit and mental toughness to avoid binge eating.

Chapter 3: Building Good Habits and Breaking Bad Ones

"If you are going to achieve excellence in big things, you develop the habit in little matters. Excellence is not an exception, it is a prevailing attitude."

(Colin Powell)

Maybe you have heard somewhere back in the day that it takes 60 days to form a new habit. Perhaps you may have heard of a different theory—and this one's shorter—that it takes 21 days to form a new habit.

Sometimes there are longer days like the 20-80 theory, and sometimes they say it takes 24 or 25 days to form a new habit. Well, that is an old science that has since been debunked.

It's not that they are not completely true. It's just that their data isn't as complete as we have it now. Studies on habit formation have grown in the past decade, and we now understand them better than we did years ago.

What experts are saying now is that there is no fixed time frame for anyone to form a new habit. It is different for everyone. According to a study [9] published in the *European Journal of Social Psychology*, it ranges from 18 days to 254 days.

The same study points out that there are 66 days to form a new habit. Well, that is the average. That is also why some theorized that it takes that long. However, that is only the average rate.

It doesn't follow that everyone needs 60 days or so. Some people may even require less, which is why some say you need 25 or 27 days to form a new habit. If you dig into the details, it takes 66 days (on average) ***for a new habit to become automatic***.

What it means is that you may already have formed a new habit before that prescriptive two-month time frame. The actual time to form the habit will rely on different factors. Sometimes it has something to do with the person wanting the new habit, and at times the new habit you want to form will affect your success rate.

We'll go into the details a little later on.

The Little Habits That Make Up Your Day

Whether you realize it or not, you already have lots of habits that you perform every day. A habit is an automatic behavior that we all do without thinking. We may not even remember creating these habits.

Here are a few routines you might want to check just to see which ones are already habitual:

- Which shoe or sock do you put on first, the left one or the right?
- How do you put your kids to bed?
- How do you feed your pet dog or cat?
- How do you take your dog out for a walk?
- When putting on a shirt, which sleeve do you start with?
- How do you wash your hair?
- How do you water your plants?
- When you mow the lawn, where do you start?
- What exercise do you start with?
- How do you start your day at work?
- How do you go shopping for essentials?
- How do you do your laundry?

- What's the first thing you do when you get home from work?
- How do you brush your teeth? How do you put toothpaste on your brush? Where do you start brushing?

The list goes on, and before you know it, you already have a long list of habits that have become a natural part of your routine. Almost everything is a habit from how you sit at your work desk to how you sit on the couch to watch Netflix.

It also includes how you react when you see your friends or how you respond when your boss sounds angry or upset. We carry out these habits without thinking about them, and we only notice them when we pay attention—like putting them in a list.

Ivan Pavlov and Classical Conditioning

Our understanding of habits, classical conditioning, and everything else connected to them started with the theories and discoveries by

Ivan Pavlov [10]. Believe it or not, it all started with studies related to saliva.

Pavlov won the Nobel Prize for his work on medicine in the year 1904. But his work started as an experiment to figure out how much saliva a dog would produce as a digestive response—totally unrelated to behavior and habit formation.

Long story short, what he discovered then formed the foundation of our understanding of classical conditioning. Pavlov found out that a dog would salivate to food, but a canine would also salivate to the footsteps of the pet owner or even the sound of the bell that announced that food was being brought to him.

The initial stimulus was the food, and the resulting behavior was the dog salivating. But then he added a second stimulus—the sounding of a bell. So each time food was being brought to the dog, a bell was chimed.

The dog would salivate and then receive the food. Pavlov then removed the first stimulus—the food. And then he would just ring the bell to see if the dog would salivate as much without the presence of the food.

The result was that the dog still salivated to the sound of the bell minus the food. You get the same response with the associated stimulus.

But you might think that hey—we're smarter than dogs, right?

Of course we are. But just like our canine friends, we humans are also creatures of habit. We also have that stimulus–response process going on within us.

Here's a classic example.

A smoker habitually lights a cigarette as soon as he sees one. The first stimulus is seeing a pack of cigarettes—it doesn't have to be his. It may be just a cigarette shown in a commercial on TV or a billboard, or even someone else who happened to be in the same smoking room as he was.

When he sees a cigarette, he would reach for his own cigarette and light it up. Now, a second stimulus can enter any time. A good example of that is boredom. Let's say a man is a smoker who is waiting for his girlfriend to get off work.

He's been waiting for an hour (he didn't know his girlfriend was doing overtime work). He's already bored, and then he sees a poster of a cigarette—of course he reaches for one and lights it.

Now, this happens several times. He gets bored exactly while seeing a cigarette. He lights it. It will eventually turn into a habit that every time he gets bored he has associated that boredom to lighting a cigarette.

This happens a lot, and it happens to everyone.

It doesn't have to be about lighting cigarettes. It can be for any habit that we form.

The Three-Step Loop in Habit Formation

Charles Duhigg and other researchers, such as BJ Fogg, for instance, have identified a three-step pattern when it comes to habit formation. They call it by different names—well, each author does.

For instance, Duhigg calls it the Cue, Routine, Reward cycle, or process. On the other hand, others would refer to it as the three Rs of Habit

Change. Well, whatever they choose to call it, just remember that they're all referring to the same thing.

I'll just use the 3 Rs because it's easier to remember. So, what are these three steps? They're the following:

1. Reminder
2. Routine
3. Reward

Reminder: This refers to the trigger or stimulus that solicits a behavior (remember Pavlov's experiment?). This trigger or cause is Duhigg's first step called the cue—well, it's pretty much the same thing. Just remember that the reminder or first step is something that will solicit a reaction.

Routine: This refers to the actual behavior that you do in response to the reminder or cue. It can be any action that you take as long as it is your response to the stimuli, cue, or reminder (again, remember they're the same thing).

A routine, therefore, is any behavior that we automatically perform every time we get a trigger or stimulus. This routine can become something that we do without even thinking about it.

Reward: The reward phase refers to the benefit that we gain from doing the behavior as a response to the trigger. Something doesn't become a habit without any reason to repeat doing it again.

The reward, in effect, reinforces the behavior as a favorable response towards the stimuli. In Pavlov's experiment, it is the food that represents the reward after the dog behaves favorably in response to the stimuli (the bell, footsteps, etc.). The dog's behavior (salivating) is reinforced by the reward and thus etching the entire routine into the mind, and it becomes a very powerful memory.

Well, it's actually more than a powerful memory. That is because if repeated enough times, it already becomes a habit. After the routine has been rewarded, everything cycles back to step 1—every time the reminder is provided, the mind automatically moves to step 2 and then step 3 in the process.

How The Three-Step Loop Works

Here's a very common and very simple example of how this three-step loop works. This cycle happens to everyone—as long as you own a phone, you may have already fallen for this cycle.

Phase 1: Phone Rings Either Text or Call (The Reminder or Trigger)

Now, this is a very common trigger. When people's phones ring, what's the very first thing they do instinctively? Yes, they reach for their phone. It doesn't matter where it is; we all reach for that phone, albeit instinctively.

It can be in our pockets, our bags, or on the bedside nightstand while you're fast asleep. When that phone rings, you reach for it. The question is: why are we mercilessly under the influence of these phones and are compelled to react?

We react because we have been conditioned to react to it. In short, we have formed the habit of answering phones promptly. We will drop everything else just to answer the said phone.

So, what serves as the trigger or cue?

Your smartphone or iPhone employs two or three cues to grab your attention. It uses a visual cue—it lights up even in the dark, it then displays the caller (a picture or maybe just a phone number), it will then create an auditory cue—it will ring, and finally, depending on the settings you choose, it will also vibrate, which is something that you will feel in case you have the phone in your pocket.

It uses a multi-sensory cue that can snatch your attention if you are not careful.

Phase 2: We Answer the Call or Text (Routine or Response)

The next phase is almost inevitable. Well, there's a way to break this habit, but we'll go over that later in this chapter. We grab our phones and answer it (text or call) sometimes automatically.

It would appear as if we have no choice—but we do. Have you ever experienced being in the middle of an interview, and you forget to put your phone on silent mode, and then it rings? Almost like some kind of lightning instinct, you forget that you're in the middle of an interview (or a business meeting or something where answering your phone is considered rude), and you almost reach for it to answer the darn thing.

But then you remember where you are and what you are doing so you just turn your phone off. It's not that the phone has any power over you, but it's just that you have made it a habit to answer your phone right then and there without question.

Phase 3: You Find Out Who It Was That Called/Texted You (The Reward)

This is the satisfaction that you get out of reacting to your phone. You can call this some kind of feedback loop. When you are satisfied during phase 3, it feeds your desire to repeat the process from the beginning.

You can compare it to a powerful reminder or memory that's telling you to answer the phone next time it rings because, according to your previous experience, you get the satisfaction from that call or text.

Experts posit that all habits that we form—whether they are complex or simple ones—follow this same three-step cycle.

Big Actions vs. Small Specific Actions

Here's an interesting question: which actions that we decide to make have a better chance of becoming a habit? Experts say it is the small specific actions that we do that have a better chance of becoming a habit.

What you need to do is to make your target habit as specific as possible. For example, let's say you made a resolution to exercise more this year. Does it ever happen? It doesn't, right?

The reason behind that is the fact that this decision to make a new exercise habit is too general and vague. If the actions you decide upon fall in that category, then they will become less likely to be adopted as a new habit.

Select your target action/habit to be as specific as it can be. In this example—exercising—you can differentiate your actual target habit like this:

- I will put on my running clothes and go on a quick jog as soon as I get home each day from work.

That is specific enough. Here's another way to formulate your newly selected habit:

- I will go on a walk every Monday, Wednesday, and Saturday morning until the following Christmas.

What You Can Do: Pick a habit. If it is too general, then specify what you want to do and when you should do it. Specify how frequently you are going to do it and how exactly you will do it. You may also create a plan on how you can get it all done.

Easy and Simple Actions vs. Complex Actions

If the planned or selected habit is too complex, chances are it won't be converted into a regular habit that you will have on your list. Other than being specific about the habit, you shouldn't choose complex habits.

For example, setting up a home gym complete with all the state-of-the-art exercise equipment and weights that you can find won't get you exercising. You'll just end up wasting a lot of money on a home gym system.

On the other hand, the very simple reminder of putting your running shoes by your bedroom door where you are sure to see it as soon as you change your work clothes is a sure reminder and trigger to your mind that you should go out to run.

What You Can Do: Pick simple habits. Remember that you can use small habits to remind you of other habits. One thing can lead to another. The simpler the habit you select, the better.

Physical Actions vs. Mental or Emotional States/Decisions

Some people think that they can make it a habit to choose to be happy no matter what happens. And then they get depressed. I have seen that happen to friends of mine. They thought they could will themselves into happiness and positivity.

The chances of success of that endeavor are very slim at best. But here's a better way to do that. Select a habit that requires any physical action that will result in making you happy.

This one, I have tried myself. I remember back in the day that I used to have fun playing tennis. So I decided that maybe I could try playing it again. All I did was bring out my old tennis racket and placed it right by the door.

That way every day I saw the old tennis racket. I didn't pick up on tennis right away, but the constant reminder because of that racket eventually allowed me to go out one afternoon to play tennis.

It happened now and then at first. But then it became something fun and then a little while later I was regularly playing tennis during the weekend all over again. Habits take time to form, but simple and actual physical actions tend to get remembered a lot better than just saying it or trying to keep things inside your head.

Okay, let's use a simpler example. I'm not very good at remembering things, so when I try to get groceries or have stuff that I need to do on certain days, I tend to forget a thing or two—and that would eventually make me upset at the end of the day.

My first solution to this problem was to take five minutes each morning and try to remember everything that I need to do. Of course, that never worked.

My second solution (which I tried a day or two later) was to buy a small notebook—one that could fit in my pocket. Along with that I also bought a pen to go with the notebook.

All I had to do was to write down all the stuff I needed to get and do on that day each morning. I also had to keep the notebook with me all day. And it worked.

Every morning I would update my list. The mere presence of the notebook was a reminder to me that I had a list. Whenever I had the chance, I checked out my list and got things done without missing an item.

Using Visual and Auditory Cues

Again, this goes back to the mobile phone analogy that we covered earlier. Auditory and visual cues create a conditioned response. Let that be a rule of thumb: if you want a new behavior to become a habit, then make sure to practice it with auditory or visual stimuli. We will go over the details about this a little later in this chapter.

Building Habits That Stick

Plato once said that "We are what we repeatedly do. Excellence then, is not an act, but a habit." The key to making an action a habit is repetition, according to that quote from the ancient philosopher.

On the outset, repetition might get the initial emphasis on everyone's mind. However, if you think about it, there is another underlying principle that Plato was trying to highlight.

You see, you can't just keep repeating something religiously without another guiding principle behind it. The true principle that will push you to keep repeating something over and over again until the action becomes ingrained in you is called *discipline*.

This is true of actions that aren't always pleasant—like fasting, exercising, restraint, and others. The immediate reward isn't always there, and you may get discouraged along the way as you try to repeat the actions associated with these goals.

That is why habits can sometimes be hard to build. In our day-to-day life, we will have a lot of distractions that can set us off our desired path. Here are five tactics that you can do to make new habits that will stick with you for a long time.

Tactic #1: Mini-Goals and Micro Quotas

Studies show that setting smaller goals can help people change their lives for the better [11]. If you have a huge habit in mind—like losing weight, for instance—you can break it down into several smaller habits (aka goals).

For instance, you can break it down into:

1. Work with a fitness coach every Saturday morning

2. Try intermittent fasting twice a week (Tuesdays and Fridays)
3. Reduce sugar intake by implementing a low-carb meal plan

By going through this goal-setting process, you will be better able to transform new behaviors into habits. Smaller goals are more realistic, and the more specific they are, the easier they are to convert into a habit.

These mini-goals will serve as your micro quotas. In other words, they represent the minimum amount of work that you have to do. It's like breaking down a huge task into smaller, doable tasks.

Every time you hit a micro quota, it gives you a sense of accomplishment. It is a self-rewarding system that encourages you to move forward and to keep repeating the task or action.

You can set these mini-goals or micro quotas daily, weekly, bi-weekly, or some other frequency that suits your needs.

Now you might be wondering if this really works. You need to look no further than writer and app developer Nathan Berry. He made a simple goal every day, and it was a commitment that changed his career.

What commitment/goal was that? It was to write 1,000 words every day. It is a tough grind, right? He made that goal back in 2012 and it skyrocketed his career. It empowered him to earn $30,000 in just a month and a half [12].

It was a mini-goal that eventually led to the accomplishment of a much larger goal. And it started with just a little habit of writing a thousand words each day.

Tactic #2: Use Behavior Chains

One of the techniques that experts have found to be quite useful in making habits stick is using behavior chains [13]. It's a very easy concept. You don't have to be taken aback by the term—it just sounds fancy.

The idea is that one behavior or action can lead to another. It makes use of physical contextual cues to remind a person of something that he or she has to do. This goes back to placing, or even hanging, your running shoes right at the door so it's the first thing you see when you walk in.

It reminds you that you should go out for a run or jog as soon as you get home. Here's another thing that worked for me. I purchased a small green bowl along with a smaller spoon.

Every night before going to bed, I would put all of that on the breakfast table on top of a placemat at the chair where I usually sit for breakfast. What it did is that every morning when I rush to prepare my breakfast cereal and milk, those things would remind me to practice portion control.

That way, I don't overeat during breakfast. Doing that until it became a habit eventually contributed to achieving my weight loss goals. Determine a small behavior or habit that you can do to achieve a bigger goal that you want to achieve.

Tactic #3: Visualize Your Goal the Right Way

You may have heard of dream boards and visualization exercises where people try to envision what they want to achieve. They may even create a pinboard and add to it anything and everything that they want for themselves.

These are visualization techniques that are designed to help you achieve your goal. However, some people are more successful in using them, and others aren't. Why is that? This is true of habits as well.

For example, if you want to visualize yourself as being able to end a smoking habit, sometimes that visualization is not enough. The same is true for other things like a brand new car, being physically fit, being financially free, and others.

You see, it is one thing to visualize what you want and take five minutes each day to do it. However, if you do not visualize the reason why you want that change to happen, then there is an essential part of the entire vision that is missing.

The reason why you have that vision should also be part of the vision as well. Going back to our example, if you envision yourself quitting smoking in six months, you should include in that vision why you want to quit.

Studies show that visualizing results alone is not enough [14]. It may even prevent you from breaking a new habit or starting a new one. So don't just visualize what you want, envision why you want what you want.

Other than the why you should also envision how you will attain it. Let's say you envision yourself making a million dollars in the next two years. Well, don't just imagine yourself with a brand new car and a paycheck with that much money.

Envision how you're going to do it. Studies from UCLA have shown that this is a more effective way to acquire a new habit and to realize a goal [15].

Visualizing and planning helps you stay focused on the new habit or goal that you want to achieve. Itemizing each step that you need to take reduces the anxiety that may come due to being unsure of what you ought to do and how to determine if you're progressing or not.

Tactic #4: Take Away Excess Options (Don't Overplan)

Research shows that having too many options when forming a new habit will deplete your mental energy [16]. The same study also points out that making repeated or multiple decisions also have the same effect.

Even if those decisions are small or mundane, they will add up and eventually take a toll on your mental faculties. So, how do you reduce the number of decisions that you have to make?

The solution suggested by experts from the Harvard Business Review is to turn the mundane and daily decisions that we make into routines [17]. Former US President Barack Obama used this strategy by just wearing gray or blue suits.

He said, *"I'm trying to pare down decisions. I don't want to make too many decisions about what I'm eating or wearing because I have too many other decisions to make."*

So how do you put this into practice? Here are a couple of ideas:

- Pack the same lunch every day for a week (just change the menu every week) so that you won't have to think about what to eat at lunchtime.
- If you have too many shoes, then just pick two or three that you really like and then

sell the others in a garage sale or give them away to charity.
- Don't go to the lunchroom or the vending machine down the hall so you won't be overwhelmed by the snack options—pack your own healthy snacks before going to work.

Note that by simplifying your choices, the better the chances that the new behavior will become a habit.

Tactic #5: Don't Give Up When You Screw Up

Do you beat yourself up inside when you make a mistake? Don't do it. Remember that each mistake is a lesson learned, and it only wafts you closer to a much-desired outcome. Think along these famous lines from Samuel Beckett:

> *"Ever tried, ever failed. No matter. Try again, fail again. Fail better."*

Take note that new habits that you form are such fragile things. That also means you should remove any possible obstacle that may lead you astray. Do you find yourself abandoning ship when you slip up the first few times?

Some people doubt themselves and think that they can't get the new habit into their system when faced with failures every now and then. Remember that each failure is a lesson, and if you scrutinize how you failed, you can identify the factors that led to that failure.

Fine-tune the screwup. Find out where you made the mistake and then try again. Don't give up.

Now you know how to grow into good habits; in the next section of this chapter, we will go over how to get rid of bad habits.

Why Habit-Building is Essential to Self-Discipline

Remember that discipline can be built on the small habits that you do every day. Micro quotas, behavior chains, visualization, simplifying goals, and a positive attitude are small habits that contribute to the establishment of better discipline.

To be a better-disciplined entrepreneur, you should acquire habits like learning a new subject or skill regularly, reading an entire book each week, being on time for appointments, networking on purpose, and finding ways to improve customer relationships.

How to Quit Bad Habits

Your good habits will help you live a better and more disciplined life. You will have more self-control if your habits are truly beneficial. But what if you have bad habits? How can you break them?

We'll go over the answers to that question and several tips along the way in this section of the chapter.

Top 10 Bad Habits

Figuring out what the top 10 bad habits are shouldn't be that difficult. Just pull up your browser and Google it. Here are the top results that I was able to find recently. Some of the results were kind of surprising.

Here's what I got (your results may be a bit different though):

- Alcohol
- Procrastination
- Smoking
- Watching TV (I was like—really???)

- Picking your nose (ugh!)
- Swearing
- Biting fingernails
- Drinking lots of coffee
- Overeating
- Playing with hair
- Worrying about things
- Late-night snacking/raiding the fridge
- Skipping breakfast

Okay, so my list is slightly longer than ten items. Note that I didn't arrange them in any particular order. I just typed them as they appeared on my search results. I had no intention of ranking them from 1 to 10.

Also, I didn't put drugs on the list because it is an addiction, and it is more than just a bad habit. Well, I guess we can remove smoking and drinking from this list, but only if they are chronic conditions that one is already experiencing.

Breaking Bad Habits

In this section, we'll go over the different methods that you can use to overcome bad habits. You can try the tips that I will mention below chronologically, or you can just pick the ones that you think are much easier for you. Note that I have arranged them in a bit of a logical order.

Identify the Reward

Remember that it was mentioned earlier when we discussed the three Rs of habit formation that every behavior that becomes a habit will have a reward associated with it. The reward reinforces the behavior, which is why it becomes habitual.

If you are nurturing a bad habit, that means you are receiving a reward for that habit. There will be a reward somewhere in some way. From behavioral psychology, we understand that habits can either be rewarded or punished.

When a behavior is rewarded, it is reinforced and may become habitual. But if a behavior is punished, then it is curbed and has a slimmer chance of becoming a habit. Rewards reinforce, while punishment reduces the chances of having that behavior repeated.

For instance, if you are a smoker, identify the reason why you smoke. What do you get out of that behavior? A lot of people smoke because it is their way to release the tension and stress that they are feeling.

When you overeat, your reward could be the taste of the food. If you have a bad habit of putting tasks off (procrastination), then your reward could be the extra free time. Identify the reward.

After identifying the automatic reward that you get for your bad habit, the next step is to decide whether to get a punishment for the habit or to remove the reward you're getting for that habit.

Punishment vs. Reward Removal

After identifying the reward you're getting for that bad habit, you have the choice of either removing that reward or just punishing the bad habit. The idea is to cut the cycle habit formation so that the bad habit won't get reinforced.

Note that this will require a certain commitment from you. You need to commit to either impose a punishment every time you do that habit or take away that reward that you are getting every time you experience a relapse.

For instance, if you are trying to lose weight and then you overeat (i.e., your bad habit) you can impose a penalty which takes away the satisfaction (i.e., the reward) of the bad habit— let's say that you commit to not have dessert until tomorrow at lunchtime or for 24 hours.

But in case you decide you want to impose a punishment for the bad habit well, here's a suggestion. Next time you overeat, then you should go on a 15-minute workout session.

Replacing the Bad Habit

Bruce Lee, the renowned martial artist and actor, once said:

"Empty your cup so that it may be filled; become devoid to gain totality."

What does that mean? It means that if your mind is already preoccupied with something, then don't expect that you will be able to fill it with something else.

The same is true when you want to learn a new habit, but a bad habit is getting in the way. What you can do is to get rid of the bad habit first and then replace it with a good one.

You are then hitting two birds with one stone. You are breaking a bad habit and getting a new and better one. The first step was to identify what reward you are getting from your bad habit—e.g., stress relief, great taste in your mouth, etc.

What you need to do is to find a replacement habit that also gives you the same or equivalent reward. It's like getting all the good out of your previous habits minus the side effects.

So, for example, your habit is that you put off your tasks for later (i.e., procrastination). The reward you are getting from this is that you get a few extra minutes to yourself to get some peace and quiet before tackling a very difficult task.

What replacement should you use? Here's a good idea—use a Pomodoro Timer. Using a Pomodoro Timer (also known as a tomato timer), you can set a very realistic work schedule that allows you to take plenty of breaks in between tasks. That way, you have more chances to do something enjoyable and reduce the tensions that your work may be having on you.

Tell a Friend

Telling a friend about a habit that you want to obtain already imposes a possible punishment or penalty for not achieving it. If we don't follow through and our friends know about it, then we are punished by the shame of failure.

Of course, the shame of it all isn't a powerful motivator. However, it may be quite effective for others. But there is another benefit that you can gain from telling others.

If you tell your goal habits to your friends, then you gain the support of the people who care. Let's say that you tell your friends that you intend to break your bad habit of swearing.

You may have times when you're so pissed off and your friends are around. Before you blurt out your next cuss word, they can give you that warning look. It's a little check and balance that you get, and because you have friends around you that are there to help you, you can slowly but surely curb the instinct to swear.

Another way to make this work is to find a buddy who also has the same problem who may also want to stop just like you. So let's say you want to quit drinking beer. Find a drinking buddy who also wants to quit.

You will then hang out, and in case either of you feels the urge, you can call one another or just send out text messages. You can then go hang out for a no-beer get-together. If someone relapses, there shouldn't be any mocking involved.

You go out and encourage each other in case a relapse happens. The support system you get from friends and buddies helps to reinforce you through the ordeal of getting rid of the bad habit. They help you get over relapses and get you on the right track again.

Friends help to reinforce your motives to stay self-disciplined. Sometimes we all need a helping hand.

Small and Big Rewards

Rewards have a huge impact on our brains. The first thing you should do when you put off a bad habit is to reward yourself. Experts suggest that you shouldn't restrict the rewards to sporadic big-time rewards.

For instance, you want to break the bad habit of living an inactive lifestyle. You can schedule a reward, such as a brand new set of gym clothes, after working out in the gym for four weeks. But four weeks is a long time, and you might end up relapsing within the first week.

What you can do is set up small rewards every time you go to the gym. You can get a protein-rich meal after gym time. Well, you need the protein anyway so that your body can recover from all the exercise that you just did.

Make a reward schedule. Use small rewards for smaller achievements, and then after a set period of time, you can schedule a big reward.

Is It a Habit or Is It an Addiction?

Now, here is a serious question. At one point, you will have to identify whether your bad habit is either just a bad habit or is it already an addiction. Because if it is already an addiction, then you will need some direct medical intervention.

Knowing the difference will help save you from a lot of frustration. Examples of addictive habits include gambling, alcohol, and smoking. Note that these habits are very difficult to break.

To determine whether you're dealing with an ordinary habit or a full-blown addiction, please answer the following question:

If I break this habit, will it cause any changes to my physique and my mentality?

Why answer that question? When you go through the process of breaking an addiction, you will undergo withdrawal symptoms. These symptoms are physiological and very noticeable. Here are the symptoms to look out for:

1. Vomiting
2. Nausea
3. Sweating
4. Shaking

You may need the help of a professional to break an addiction. It will require more than just your effort to get over one. If that is the case, please see immediate medical help.

Breaking Bad Habits to Improve Self-Discipline

Bad habits impede self-mastery, and they are hindrances to self-discipline. To increase your productivity and achieve better self-discipline, you must get rid of any bad habits that you may have picked up along the way.

How to Practice Delayed Gratification and How to Overcome Temptations

One of the most powerful ways to gain impulse control and to improve self-discipline is to practice delayed gratification. What is delayed gratification, and how can you use that to increase your self-mastery? We'll answer that question and more in this section.

What is Delayed Gratification?

Delayed gratification involves the ability to wait for any given amount of time before you can get what it is that you want [18]. Delayed gratification can be a bit difficult for some people, while others have the ability to do it whenever they want.

If you want a more technical definition, here's a brief one:

"Delayed gratification is the ability to postpone an immediate gain in favor of greater and later reward."

Imagine this scenario. You're at a party with your friends, and they bring out all the delicious-looking and nice-smelling scrumptious food. Unfortunately, you're trying to lose weight.

You have two options—give in and enjoy all the food with your friends or just pick the healthy options and stay on your diet and still enjoy the company of your friends. It is the gratification of your senses versus your willpower to stay on a diet.

If you manage to just stick to the salads and maybe a few carrot sticks, then you still get to enjoy the company of friends and eventually lose weight, which is your long-term goal. Does that mean you will never get to enjoy tasty party food ever?

Of course not—you will still get to enjoy that kind of food, but not today.

Your satisfaction with being able to eat like a king will be given to you the day you hit your fitness goals. Once you create a good habit of exercising and eating healthy, you can allow occasional "cheat days." You are essentially delaying the gratification of your senses until that day when you achieve what you want to achieve.

Now imagine your reward if you stay away from the party food this time around: you will be in better shape, look great, and you can occasionally allow yourself to eat more of the great food without feeling guilty and still look great while others look on in envy at your figure.

Now the question is, will you trade what is right before you now for what you can become and have in the future?

And that is basically at the heart of delayed gratification.

It All Began with a Marshmallow

Our understanding of delayed gratification began with the Stanford Marshmallow Experiment. You may have seen videos about this experiment on YouTube, or you may have seen the video as part of an ad on TV.

This experiment was conducted back in 1972 by Walter Mischel. And this is how the experiment went:

- It all began by bringing a child (sometimes two) into a room with a table at the center and a chair to sit on. A plate with a marshmallow was placed in front of the child.
- After placing the treat where the child can see it and, of course, reach for it at will, the researcher would then make a deal. The deal was that the researcher was going to leave the room and return some time later.
- The child (or children) is allowed to eat the marshmallow if they wanted to. However, if the child waited, then the researcher will bring another marshmallow—sort of a reward for waiting.
- Now, here's the catch. If the child ate the first marshmallow, the deal is that the researcher won't give another marshmallow.
- Some of the kids played with the marshmallow until, eventually, they gave in to the temptation. Other kids grabbed the marshmallow as soon as the door

closed behind the researcher. Some kids were able to refrain from eating the marshmallow, and thus they were given a second treat.

The researchers observed the kids as they grew up and found that those who were able to control themselves fared better later in life. They even had better SAT scores. This experiment and the said video with the kids became quite popular back in the day.

Of course, that was only the initial study on the theory of delayed gratification. There were follow-up studies too [19].

What the researchers back in the 1970s discovered then led to a whole new understanding of the power of delayed gratification. There were other follow-up studies conducted on the same children who participated as well [20]. These and other studies also helped us understand the factors involved in delayed gratification [21].

Practical Benefits of Delayed Gratification

You don't have to participate in any science experiment just to see the potential benefits of delayed gratification. You can already imagine how it might help you out if you just practiced a little more self-control.

Here are a couple of examples:

- An example of practicing delayed gratification is when a student commits to finishing all his homework first before watching Netflix. Once all of that is done, the student can watch Netflix for the rest of the day. All the important tasks get done, the student can expect to get better grades and have more time to enjoy his favorite shows.
- By choosing not to use your credit card to buy the latest iPhone, you practice delayed gratification. You take on a disciplined approach instead by putting some money aside so you can pay for it in cash.

The practical application of this principle is that you choose to be disciplined first and put distractions behind you. In effect, you are choosing between the easy way out and the hard but more rewarding way.

What Determines Your Ability to Practice Delayed Gratification

Before you can better practice the principle of delayed gratification, you should first understand the factors that contribute to your capability to do it. As it turns out, your experiences and the environment have a huge impact on your ability to forego immediate satisfaction (i.e., delayed gratification).

Researchers from the University of Rochester replicated the marshmallow experiment but added a very important detail [22]. Other than the marshmallow, the kids were either given stickers or crayons as well.

The researcher then promised to give more or better crayons or stickers. Some of the kids were made to wait in vain, and the researcher never fulfilled her promise of more/better crayons or stickers. But some of the kids were given new crayons/stickers a few minutes later.

After that came the marshmallows. Researchers found out that the kids who had negative experiences with the researcher (she never fulfilled her promise of more/better crayons or stickers) were more likely to be unable to practice delayed gratification compared to those who experienced the researcher fulfilling her promises.

Researchers found out that they could sway a child either to practice delayed gratification or not depending on their initial experience with the researcher. If they found out that the researcher was reliable, then they would be more willing to wait and not eat the marshmallow that was on the plate before them.

What researchers learned here is that the ability to delay gratification is not an inherent trait. No one is born with this ability to discipline themselves in such a way. Sure, some are better than others at first. But it only proves that people can learn it. It can be influenced by one's experiences and also the surrounding environment.

Each child who participated in this experiment learned two things:

1. They have the capability to wait for a better reward
2. If they waited for a later gratification of what they wanted, then the end result is worth it

How to Get Better at Delayed Gratification and Overcoming Temptations

The good news is that anyone can get better at delayed gratification. That also means that anyone can get better at resisting temptations and practicing self-control. Just remember that everyone has the ability to do it.

Here are some of the things that you can do to improve:

Start Small

Make the new habit very easy to do so that it is impossible for you to say no. For example, if you hardly exercise, then make it a habit to do jumping jacks every day in the morning for only two minutes—no more, no less.

You want to cut back on drinking soda and sweet drinks? Then make it a habit to skip drinking sodas only on Mondays. You want to start a writing habit but have no gusto to write an entire novel? Then start by writing three-sentence blog posts every day. Keep doing it until it becomes habitual.

Start small. Once you have made that into a habit, then move on to bigger things. At least now you know that you have the power to exercise delayed gratification.

Find Out What is Holding You Back

There was a time when I defined myself as a person who hated working out. I thought I was destined to become out of shape forever. That was until the time when I realized that I needed to live a healthier lifestyle.

I spoke to a fitness coach who was wise enough to probe through my excuses. We found out that I didn't hate exercising. After some serious introspection, the real reason why I didn't like working out is that I didn't feel comfortable about exercising in public.

The thought of seeing other fit and muscular guys outperforming me at the gym frightened me. The bottom line was that I was embarrassed at how I looked being flabby and all.

The solution that was suggested to me made sense—work out at home. I started with yoga videos. Eventually, after a few months, a free yoga class was offered in school, so I went there.

I was able to attend that class because I thought to myself, *At least I'm exercising with people I know*. The gym was different because the people there were all strangers to me. From school yoga I was able to transition into the gym after being comfortable exercising with and in front of other people.

The secret to all of this was finding out the real reason why you can't do what you were supposed to. Dig deep into your excuses.

Expect to Fail and Create a Plan When You Fail

"You're not good enough to be disappointed"—that is from strength and conditioning coach Dan John. When you are new at something, do you think you're already good at it so much that you ought to be disappointed when you fail at it?

Of course not—that means you shouldn't get disappointed when you experience failure since you're not even that good at delayed gratification. Expect to fail. You should expect that you will give in to temptation.

What you should be doing is to prepare a plan to pick yourself up when you do fail. Here are a few ideas:

1. Forget about deadlines; set schedules instead and monitor your progress.
2. Focus on building your new you (i.e., how good you are at delaying gratification) and don't stress out about how fast or slow you are progressing.
3. Never miss two times in a row. What this means is that you may fail once in a while, but once you are aware of the failure, you will want to avoid repeating the same

mistake in a row. This prevents you from forming the habit again.

Focus on the Process Not the Performance

Here's a strategy used by the great Jerry Seinfeld: make a commitment to do something that will require you to practice delayed gratification. It can be anything from not having dessert at lunch to not drinking soda. Anything will be great.

Now, print a calendar for that month and hang it by a mirror. Or tape it on the wall right next to the mirror. That way, you see it every day. Each day before you go to bed, mark that day on the calendar with an "X" if you were able to meet your commitment to delay gratification.

After you've been at it, you will notice that you will have some X days on that calendar. Next time you try it, here's what you're going to do—each day, when you've achieved marking an X on that calendar, try to create a chain of Xs.

You were able to do it on Monday, so try your very best to succeed so that you can put an X on Tuesday, and so on. Create a chain and then try not to break the chain. Just focus on making the chain longer and maintaining it.

Don't worry about how well you did. What matters is that you were able to do it. If it is about exercising every day, then don't worry if you only exercise for five minutes or two minutes. The important thing is that you exercised.

Focus on not breaking that chain. Keep at it until whatever commitment you made has become habitual.

Sturgeon's Law and the Pareto Principle

Sturgeon's Law is named after science fiction author Theodore Sturgeon [23]. He coined the saying, "Ninety percent of science fiction is crud, but then, ninety percent of everything is crud." Back in 1951, he called it Sturgeon's Revelation, but everybody just called it Sturgeon's Law instead.

A simplified version of what he said is, "Nothing is always absolutely so." If you prefer having numbers in it, then just stick with the 90% of everything is crap.

Now, the idea behind Sturgeon's Law is similar to another maxim called the Pareto Principle, which is also known as the 80/20 rule—the law of the vital few. A simplified definition of the Pareto Principle is this: 80% of the effects that anyone produces are derived from 20% of the causes.

The Pareto Principle is named after Vilfredo Pareto [24]. Pareto observed that 80% of the wealth of Italy only belonged to 20% of the population. People have observed this to be true in many things as well, such as:

- 20% of input produces 80% of output
- 20% of a product's features produces 80% of its usage
- 20% of all the workers produce 80% of the results
- You only watch 20% of all the channels on cable TV, and you spend 80% of your total viewership on those few channels

As you can see, the only difference between the Pareto Principle and Sturgeon's Law is the percentages. But essentially they mean the same thing. The next question is, what do they have to do with building good habits and breaking bad ones?

The lesson here is that you should focus on the 20% (Pareto) or 10% (Sturgeon) that made a difference in your resolve. Sure, there were times when you failed, but there were times when you succeeded in maintaining a new habit (or breaking the old bad one).

Now, when you focus on the 20% or 10% that brought you the best results, it doesn't matter how much you failed. Focusing on the details of that 20% or 10% will help you produce 80% or 90% of the results later on. Study and analyze the factors that came into play for your small successes and then put them into practice.

With all of this in mind, in the next sections of this book, we will go over four essential habits that you can work on that will help you stay motivated and practice better self-discipline.

Essential Habit #1 – How to Build and Stick to a Workout Plan

If you're anything like me, then one of the hardest parts of any workout plan is showing up for gym time or getting on the road and start jogging. We sometimes think of a billion reasons why we can't go work out on any given day.

Here's an interesting strategy that you can implement to make things work for you when you work out. Here it is—make workouts a no-brainer. Studies show that it takes an average of 18 to 66 days for a habit to stick [25].

You can get that done a lot better if you turn your workouts into no-brainers. Eventually, after a good amount of tries and fails, you will put everything on autopilot.

This chapter goes over several strategies on how you can be more disciplined in your workout. The habits that you pick up from a disciplined approach to your exercise routines can also be used in the other things you do from day-to-day.

Keep It Short and Consistent

Here's a rule of thumb: it is better to have a short gym session each day than to have none. If you don't have much time, then make quality workouts instead of quantity. Ask your gym instructor about HIIT or circuit training instead.

By keeping your routines short, you can be more consistent and disciplined about your workout. It is easier to maintain discipline and consistency about smaller and simpler things. You don't need to allocate huge chunks of time to your exercise routines, and you get a sense of fulfillment because you're getting things done.

Break Things Up

Life can get hectic, and it can happen a lot. So, you can't have a 30-minute workout that day. What you can do is to break up your total workout time into three 10-minute workout chunks. You can do it this way—have 10-minute workouts before breakfast, lunch, and as soon as you get home.

That way, you achieve your goal of working out 30 minutes a day. The same can be applied to other tasks. If you have a financial report to complete, then break it down into smaller doable chunks or subtasks and get things done one subtask at a time.

Be Accountable

Exercise with a friend and agree to meet up at the gym or park (or wherever you two talked about) and go there at the set time. That way, you're also worried about not disappointing your friend. As an added bonus, you also get some quality time with your friend, which makes the routine feel enjoyable.

It will make you more disciplined because you will feel the added responsibility since you agreed to do things with someone else.

Add Variety

Doing the same thing over and over gets boring; you eventually lose focus. It's hard to stay disciplined about something if you lack focus. To get your mind back on track, you should add variety to the things that you're doing.

Try out new things because even the latest and hottest workout can become boring eventually. Try some new cardio each week, follow it up with some yoga, and maybe do some Thai boxing somewhere in your schedule. Try different things to keep you interested and motivated.

Have Fun

People like to keep doing something fun, right? Making working out fun will keep you interested and focused.

Don't be the serious grouch at the gym. Have fun working out with friends. You can turn part of your workout sessions into a kind of contest. You can even post leader boards about who can do the most reps or lift the most weight.

Essential Habit #2 – Maintain a Healthy Diet

Everyone knows that 80% of weight loss has more to do with your diet than exercise. Eating healthy doesn't only help you lose weight, but it also ensures that you have more energy during the day.

It also helps to boost your mood, and a healthy diet reduces your risk for chronic disease and reduces brain fog. However, despite all of these benefits, a lot of us still have problems maintaining and sticking to a healthy diet.

Here are some suggestions that will be helpful at staying disciplined about dieting. Making a diet stick is one of the biggest tests in self-discipline. Those who are truly disciplined about their eating habits have better mental clarity because they are healthier.

Start with Realistic Expectations

Studies have shown that when people are pressured to lose weight, they tend to fail eventually. Your plan to eat healthily will backfire when you get a lot of pressure to get results fast. Research even suggests that when you feel this pressure that you will have a higher tendency to drop out of any kind of weight loss program within a year [26].

The better alternative is to set realistic expectations. Talk with your fitness coach and set your expectations straight.

Clean Up Your Pantry/Fridge

It should be obvious that it is difficult to stick to a healthy meal plan when you are surrounded by temptation in the form of unhealthy food. The simple solution, of course, is to do an inventory of your fridge.

Clean it out. Remove the unhealthy snacks, treats, and food options. Give them away to charity or to a friend who may want them. Next, make a new grocery list full of healthy food options and then go out and buy them.

Here are some foods that nutritionists have recommended to help reduce brain fog:

- *Cocoa* – boosts overall brain power, improves memory, and helps you concentrate
- *Nutritional Yeast* – rich in B Vitamins that improves overall cognitive function
- *Turmeric* – rich in curcumin, which reduces cognitive decline
- *Spinach* – rich in lutein, which can prevent cognitive impairment
- *Eggs* – loaded with lots of choline that enhances cognition and memory
- *Avocados* – rich in Vitamin E, which has been shown to slow cognitive decline

Schedule a healthy diet meal plan. Make sure that the recipes are tasty and include recipes that you love. Being more disciplined in your food choices translates to better discipline in other aspects of your life. Best-selling author and life coach Stephen Covey explains that smaller victories translate to bigger and more fulfilling victories.

Find Out What Really Motivates You

You have to write down your goals. You may even have employed a vision board. If that is the case, then make sure to include a vision of yourself having that healthy figure.

You can even include a picture of all the healthy food that you want to eat. Write down the reasons why you want to eat a healthy diet. You can make a collage out of your vision or dream board and take a picture using your phone.

Every time you feel discouraged, or you are tempted to eat unhealthy food, then you can look at that photo and be reminded of the reasons why you wanted to eat healthy in the first place. You can even use it as the wallpaper of your phone so that it is the first picture you see when you answer a call or send out a text message.

Having a clear-cut goal will motivate you to keep going. Even if you fail sometimes, your goals will keep you committed and disciplined.

Skip the All or Nothing Mindset

Do you often think that your diet is ruined because you had some ice cream or you gave in to your cake craving? That is an all or nothing mindset and isn't going to help you.

The same is true when it comes to work and your goals. Do you call it quits when you fail to close that sale? By skipping the all or nothing mindset, you keep going despite your failures.

Everyone makes mistakes, and just because you failed that one time it doesn't mean that you have already ruined your diet—or you're a failed entrepreneur.

Forgive yourself on the spot and pick up where you left off. If you have reached your maximum calorie intake for that day because of that ice cream, then just go on with the rest of the day. Resume your diet immediately and let bygones be bygones.

Change Your Diet and Exercise Plan at the Same Time

When you try a new diet, it should be complemented by a new exercise plan. Studies suggest that when you make this tandem, your chances of success will improve since both of these changes tend to reinforce each other [27].

When two habits reinforce one another, your chances of maintaining both habits increase. *Here's an example. You want more consistent results at work—let's say you want to make it to work on time every time? Then make it a habit to get enough sleep each night so you can wake up early and refreshed every morning.*

You can also complement that with food that can help you wake up better each morning, such as apples, eggs, dark chocolate, red meat, and spinach. Making healthy food choices is a display and practice in better self-discipline. These are habits that help you become more disciplined.

Have a Healthy Snack in Your Pocket Always

Keeping a healthy snack on hand will help you avoid buying unhealthy snacks from the vending machine (or anywhere you usually buy them from). That way, when you get hungry or when you're tempted by unhealthy food options, you have something to munch on. This practice helps you stick to your health and fitness plan.

One of the best ways to stay disciplined is to avoid temptation. Are you tempted to put things off and procrastinate? Then find something that can take your mind off the temptation, like a photo of your kids or maybe a dream vacation you're saving up for. Keep it on hand so that you can be reminded of better things and resist the enticement.

Plan Ahead When You Go Out or Travel

Sticking to a healthy diet plan is easy when you're at home. You have all your healthy food options there. However, you can't say the same thing for restaurants or diners, especially when you're on the road traveling to some distant point in the country.

When you have to travel, then you should research the restaurants that serve healthy food options that you will find as you make your journey. Plan your trip so that you will make stops at those restaurants, bars, stores, or diners.

And just to make sure, in case you can't find any place that serves healthy options, then pack your own snacks and meals.

Start Your Day with a High Protein Breakfast

Starting your day with a high protein diet will reduce the chances of getting hunger pangs or cravings. Note, however, that your breakfast should be well balanced but should have more protein.

Protein takes longer to digest, and that means you will feel full for most of the day. Studies show that doing this might even help you keep your blood sugar levels steady [28]. You also tend to avoid overeating for the rest of the day as well [29].

Remember That It Takes Time to Change Your Eating Habits

How many years have you been on that unhealthy diet of yours? Was it five or maybe ten or so years? Do you think you can change that in a week? The answer is no.

It will take time before you can replace unhealthy eating habits with healthy eating habits. A lot of times, those old habits will creep up on you. And that's okay because that will happen from time to time.

What's important is that you get back to your healthy eating habits as soon as you can. Give it as much time as it needs. The important thing is that those little changes are piling up, and you are getting healthier steadily and surely.

Being healthy and making healthy food choices improves mental clarity. Your ability to focus diminishes when your brain doesn't get the nutrition it needs. Adding foods that help to reduce brain fog to your diet helps increase mental focus.

Essential Habit #3 – Sleep/Wake Up Early

Do you hit the snooze button first thing in the morning? Let me guess—you also have a zombie routine to go with it too. Getting up in the morning is usually one of the first challenges that we face.

Sometimes you just want to stay in bed just for once in your life. Sometimes you just want to get over that sleepy feeling early in the morning so you can get your day started with a lot more energy and enthusiasm.

Chances are if you feel that way most mornings, then you may be sleep-deprived. That might also mean you need to do some tweaking concerning your sleeping routine.

The good news is that there are things you can do to help you sleep well and wake up early with a lot of energy to begin your day.

Deciding to wake up early is a test of your self-discipline. By choosing to get enough sleep, sleeping early, and waking up early, you practice self-discipline first thing in the morning. You begin your day with a disciplined start.

Admiral McRaven explained that the simple act of waking up early in the morning and making his bed improved his productivity. This habit radically transformed his life.

Signs That You May Be Sleep-Deprived

Here are some of the telltale signs that you may be sleep-deprived:

- Excessive yawning
- Increased appetite
- Brain fog
- Excessive daytime sleepiness
- Fatigue
- Lack of motivation
- Irritability

Note that if you experience two or more of the symptoms mentioned above, then you may be having quality sleep problems. Being sleep-deprived is a huge factor when it comes to waking up early in the morning.

Why Is It Difficult to Wake Up in the Morning

There is more to it than just loving your bed and hating the morning. Taking medication, certain medical conditions, and lifestyle factors can sometimes make it really difficult to wake up in the morning.

Other than being sleep-deprived, there are other possible causes for why you may be having a hard time waking up in the morning. Here's a partial list of possible causes:

- Chronic pain
- Medications such as muscle relaxers, beta-blockers, and antidepressants
- Circadian rhythm sleep disorders
- Depression
- Anxiety
- Stress
- Sleep deficiency
- Sleep apnea

How to Wake Up Early in the Morning

Now there are several things that you can do to help you wake up early in the morning. However, do take note that if you do have sleep deprivation problems and other disorders, then you might need some medical intervention to address this problem.

Improve Bedtime Routines

One of the first things that you can do is to improve your routine before going to bed. If you're not doing this already, then you are, in effect, sabotaging your efforts to wake up better in the morning.

Things, like using your phone or taking caffeinated drinks, can disrupt your sleeping patterns. Cellphones emit blue light that prevents people from getting to sleep. Caffeine is a substance that will keep you alert and, of course, prevents you from sleeping.

To sleep better, you should avoid using your phone an hour before you go to bed. You should also avoid taking caffeinated drinks at a later part of the day. Here are other things that can disrupt your circadian rhythm that you should avoid:

- Drinking alcohol before bedtime
- Taking too many naps during the day

- Drinking coffee or any caffeinated drink six hours before going to bed
- Looking at screens that emit blue light before going to bed (includes phones, laptops, tablets, etc.)

Make sure to avoid these things to improve your bedtime routine. You can also sleep with the light turned off or dimmed. Use a lampshade on your bed stand to reduce the amount of light in the room when you sleep if you find it hard to sleep in the dark.

Move Your Alarm Further Away

The snooze button is truly tempting, isn't it? Getting a few more minutes of sleep can sometimes be very irresistible. But if you do that, you will just get fragmented sleep, which won't do you much good anyway.

So, here's a little suggestion—keep that alarm further away. We usually put it on the bedside table, but that is still too close for comfort. I suggest that you move your alarm all the way to the other side of the room. Place it on a chair away from your bed if you have to.

If you do it that way, then you will be forced to get up from the bed and walk over to the alarm. Sometimes that is all that is needed to get you started first thing in the morning.

Exercise Regularly

People with chronic fatigue syndrome may find it very beneficial to exercise regularly. Research suggests that it can increase energy levels, reduce fatigue, and it will also help them sleep better [30].

It can also help people sleep at night and wake up better in the morning, especially for those suffering from depression, anxiety, insomnia, and excessive sleepiness.

Get Some More Sunlight

Sunlight regulates our circadian rhythm. A healthier circadian rhythm will improve the quality of your sleep, which in turn helps you wake up earlier and with more energy in the morning.

The goal is to get some sunshine first thing in the morning. The sun does not just boost your energy levels, it also gives your mood a much-needed pick-me-up. You can also make it a morning routine to open the blinds as soon as you get up from bed.

Other than that, you can also make it a habit to take a morning walk. Another thing I suggest is to take your morning cup of coffee and enjoy it outside under the early morning sun.

But what if it is a cloudy day and the sun isn't out? The best thing you can do in that scenario is to just turn on the lights in the house.

When All Else Fails

Let's say you tried all suggestions and you still have trouble waking up early in the morning. On top of that, you also notice that you have sleep disorder signs as well. So, what do you do?

In that case, you may have to talk to your doctor and ask for a referral so you can see a sleep specialist. A sleep study can help to diagnose your sleeping disorder. This might be necessary to help you resolve symptoms of morning fatigue.

Some of the known sleep disorders include restless leg syndrome (RLS) and chronic insomnia. The type of treatment will also vary depending on the condition that you will be diagnosed with.

A sleep specialist might provide you with any of the following treatments:

- Surgery for obstructive sleep apnea
- Behavioral therapy
- A breathing device to help you stop snoring
- Melatonin therapy
- Prescription drugs for RLS and other sleep aids

By addressing the causes of sleep depravity, you sleep better and wake up better each day. Being refreshed at the beginning of the day sets you up for making better choices and a more disciplined approach to the rest of your day. You can't be mentally tough if your mind can't beat the call of your mattress.

Essential Habit #4 – Work Smart: Eat the Frog

When you hear the term "eat the frog," it can be one of the weirdest things that you will ever hear in your life. But it is one of the biggest habits that you can develop, especially when it comes to working smart.

Where Did That Phrase Come From?

The man that came up with that phrase is no other than American classical author Mark Twain. His original statement was this:

"If it's your job to eat a frog, it's best to do it first thing in the morning. And if it's your job to eat two frogs, it's best to eat the biggest one first."

No, he didn't mean to gross us out when he said that. But this is what he meant. The frog represents the worst or the most unpleasant thing you have to do during the day. It can be anything.

You hate doing that thing so much that it could be the first thing that you will procrastinate on. Simply put, what Mark Twain is suggesting is that we should prioritize the worst task on our to-do list. Well, that is giving it a more modern twist and interpretation since the concept of a to-do list wasn't available in his time.

Which is Your Biggest Frog?

As it was explained earlier, a frog represents a task that you have to do today. Now, we also mentioned that this task is the worst one that you have to do today. Well, it's not necessarily the worst thing you have ever done or will do.

When we say worst task, we mean that it is one of the most important tasks that you will have to do that day. It may be important, but it is the one among all those really important tasks that you will most likely put off.

If you can put it off until tomorrow—never mind how important it is—you will do it. You will procrastinate doing it. It can be anything from slides that your boss is waiting for, it could be a dreaded phone call that you have to make, a doctor's appointment, that annual physical, breaking up with someone, or it could be a deadline that you need to beat.

The Rationale behind the Frog-Eating Habit

Why do you have to do the worst item on your to-do list first? There should be some form of benefit behind it. Other authors and productivity experts have caught up on the idea or principle of eating the frog first [31].

One of the most well-known authors to follow suit is Brian Tracy [32]. His book *Eat That Frog,* which was published in 2006, is now a classic. He paraphrases Mark Twain slightly by saying that you should "eat your frog," which is pretty much what Twain originally meant to say.

Tracy explains that the best leaders and top executives are the ones that have made it a habit to tackle the major task first thing each working day. It should become a routine habit if you want to achieve the highest levels of productivity and performance.

Launch yourself into that major task and muster the discipline to get it done before everything else. Turn this into a daily habit, and you will have done more than any other person in the office every single day.

Too Many Meetings

Tracy notes further that one of the biggest flaws in many organizations today is that we have so many meetings. It's like we are addicted to meetings. It doesn't matter which organization you're looking at.

It happens to small businesses, medium-scale enterprises, large multimillion-dollar businesses, churches, non-profit organizations, BINGO clubs, and other organizations. We all do a lot of talking and make a lot of great plans, but only a few are getting the job done.

Dive! Dive! Dive!

The secret, Tracy explains, is to make it a habit to get into action immediately. The first thing you should do when you get into work mode is to identify your biggest frog. And within the next five minutes, you should hack into it until it is done.

No Shortcuts

Anyone who has ever cultivated this habit of eating the frog first will tell you that there are no shortcuts. You will fail to do it some days, but you just have to keep doing it every single day until it becomes a habit.

One thing they promise, though, is that when you make it a habit, this "eat the frog first principle" can be addictive. You get the most difficult task done first thing each day, and then you're all set for easy street the rest of the day.

One last thing is that at the end of the day, you should identify the frog for the following day and make a note about it that you will see as soon as you step into your work zone. That way you save time—you no longer have to sit around deciding which one is your biggest frog each day. You just dive into it as soon as you arrive at the office.

Essential Habit #5 – Mindfulness

You may have heard of mindfulness as a kind of meditation, but it is actually more than that. Yes, there is a meditative part to it, but it is also a state of mind and a habit. Apart from helping you learn to sharpen your focus, it also has a lot of other benefits.

What is Mindfulness?

Jon Kabat-Zinn [33], the man who popularized mindfulness in the West, described mindfulness in the simplest way—he described it as:

"The practice of being aware."

Note that mindfulness and mindfulness meditation are two separate things. Mindfulness is a day-to-day practice, while mindfulness meditation is a type of meditation.

Although, do take note that Kabat-Zinn also describes mindfulness as a type of meditation. The two terms get interchanged a lot, I know. Mindfulness meditation has more to do with what Buddhists practice known as *samatha*—but that is a whole different topic in itself.

You'll see the difference as we go over the details in the discussion below. For now, you can think of mindfulness as a habit, and mindfulness meditation is, of course, a type of meditation—but you get the same benefits from both.

Mindfulness is the practice (or habit) of purposefully putting your attention and focus on the things occurring in the present moment. You take everything that is happening in stride and do not apply any judgment, and accept events for what they are.

Some say that this is one of the key elements for anyone who is in search of true and lasting happiness.

Studies have shown that if this practice is done correctly, it has the power to reduce anxiety and stress [34]. It can also reduce that feeling of being overwhelmed, and it will help you to appreciate all the things that are happening around you.

You live from one moment to the other fully and wholly. It has enabled thousands to navigate an ever-changing and chaotic world. Many are using it today to help them overcome and cope with a hectic and sometimes insane schedule.

How Can You Benefit from a Mindfulness Habit?

We have already mentioned a few benefits of being mindful. We'll go over several more benefits that might convince you to adopt such a behavior.

Benefit #1: Prevents Overthinking and Anxiety

One of the symptoms of anxiety is the tendency to overthink things. When you start worrying over anything, your brain will begin to exercise a vice-like hold on such a thought. That is why sometimes it is very hard to let go of such worries.

In my experience, when I worry about something, I enter into what is known as a *thought loop.* I go through all possible bad outcomes—especially the worst-case scenario I could come up with. And then I play that back over and over in my head until it consumes me.

This isn't something healthy or useful. Going through a thought loop won't stop or prevent the terrible imagined events from happening. According to one study, people who practice mindfulness tend to reduce this frequency of rumination [35].

Another study suggests that those who practice mindfulness are able to reduce feelings of stress and anxiety [36].

Benefit #2: Improves Performance, Concentration, and Memory

Having the habit of concentrating on the task at hand improves your overall performance. It empowers you to concentrate on one thing at a time. You can learn to focus on something solely and not get distracted.

That also has another benefit; it improves one's cognitive ability. Experts are currently using this practice as a method to help people who have mind-wandering tendencies. According to research, students who practice mindfulness learn to pay attention to everything both inside the classroom and in their personal lives [37].

According to another study, it is possible that mindfulness meditation can aid in the thickening of the cerebral cortex [38]. The cerebral cortex is that part of the brain that is responsible for learning, concentration, and memory.

Benefit #3: Cognitive Flexibility

Are you easily affected by comments, news, music, media, and other things happening around you? Do you quickly react to negative criticism? If you usually find yourself losing control when something bad happens, then maybe a mindfulness habit can help you, according to one study [39].

Benefit #4: Alleviates Stress

Mindfulness as a practice and a habit can shield you from the chaos and complexity of life in our modern society. It's a buffer that you can use— you focus on what's in front of you, and your mind doesn't wander off to the worries and insecurities presented to you through your everyday experiences.

Benefit #5: Improves Sleep

Note that mindfulness meditation is a very relaxing activity. It helps people find peace and quiet in their lives. By doing this type of meditation before bedtime, people have found a way to improve the quality of their sleep.

According to one study, mindfulness meditation increases the mind's relaxation response [40]. It facilitates better control over one's autonomic nervous system—that part of your brain that is responsible for relaxation and better awareness.

Those are the top 5 benefits of a mindfulness habit. There are others, of course, like increased pain relief, promoting better mental health, improving one's sex life, fostering happy relationships, enhancing creativity, reducing the incidence of burnout, and boosting academic performance, among many others.

How to Practice Mindfulness Now

You don't have to be an expert to practice mindfulness. You may already have practiced it at least once before. Do you drive a car? Do you remember the first time you took a driving test?

Were you totally focused on driving and paying attention to the examiner's instructions? You were totally aware that the test examiner was watching you, trying to see if you were using the mirrors properly and how you handle the vehicle.

Of course, you're not expected to make small talk, but you will have to communicate with the examiner from time to time. If the weather was bad that day, you would have to tell the test examiner that you're slowing down due to weather conditions, but you were still paying attention to how you were driving.

There are other moments when you had to concentrate really hard and you were instantly super focused. You had a heightened awareness of what was going on. If you play sports, then you may have already experienced this state as well.

Now, imagine having that level of focus instinctively. You can toggle into that state at will and forget all the worries and just get things done fast and efficiently.

Here are simple steps that you can follow to practice mindfulness as a habit. After the next section, we will go over some mindfulness meditation exercises so you can practice mindfulness as a habit.

Step #1: Allocate a space and choose a time for mindfulness practice

You will need to allocate some time and a special place to practice mindfulness at first. But when you get the hang of it, you will be able to enter a mindfulness state at will. For now, dedicate both time and a place where you can do mindfulness exercises.

Dedicate a few minutes of your time each day to practice mindfulness. It should be a time when you're not rushing or when the house is peaceful. When I first did this, I set my alarm early enough so that I woke up 30 minutes ahead of everyone else in the house.

That gave me time to brush my teeth, prepare some coffee, and get comfy. I didn't ask Alexa (yes, I bought one) for any flash briefings since I had the tendency to get depressed because of the news.

I also set up a portion of the living room—a little corner by the window where the kids don't usually go to frolic and play. It has to be done in this special place so as to help trigger your mind that it is time to relax and calm down.

You can choose any time of the day you want to do your mindfulness exercise. You can do it first thing in the morning or when you get back home from work. Some practice it 30 minutes before going to bed at night. The choice is up to you.

You also get to choose how much time you want to practice mindfulness. I suggest that you start with five to ten minutes at first. And then you can extend it to 15 to 20 minutes. Now set your alarm for five or ten minutes—or whatever length of time you intended to allocate to mindfulness.

Next, after setting the time and place, go to that place at the appointed time, and sit down. Relax.

Inhale and then exhale. Repeat this until you feel calm.

Step #2: Focus and choose to do so despite distractions and challenges

It will take some effort to focus on what you are doing while you're sitting in your special space for mindfulness. Your thoughts will wander about your problems, the mistakes you made in the past, and a lot of other things that will try to grab your attention.

At this time, choose to focus on what you are doing—sitting down and trying to relax.

Inhale and then exhale—repeat this while you're seated there.

Step #3: Allow yourself that time to do nothing

Make a conscious effort to focus on what you are doing—you're sitting. You're trying to relax. Try to empty your mind and just enjoy the peace and quiet as you sit down in your special place.

Think about this—the past is long gone, and you can't do anything about it. The future is unknown to all of us, so why worry? The only thing you have absolute control over is the present. That is what you have complete control over right now.

Remember that this is a moment for your mind to recharge. Just sit there and empty your mind. Leave your worries behind. Try not to think about your problems.

Inhale and then exhale—repeat this while you're seated there.

Step #4: Try not to look at the clock

You will be tempted to look at the clock or check your phone from time to time. If you can rearrange the furniture, make sure that your back is turned away from the clock. Place your phone at a distant table, counter, or another surface. Trust that your alarm clock will go off at the designated time.

Inhale and then exhale—repeat this while you're seated there.

Step #5: Pay attention but don't judge and let it all pass

Notice that while you're trying to relax, your thoughts, memories, and feelings will creep into your mind. As you sit there looking at the wall and other things around you, a lot of things will trigger your memories.

You will recall conversations, things that you have said, experiences that you are proud of, and things that you have done that you regret to this day. What do you do when all of that crashes on you like an avalanche?

The answer is to let it all pass. Just observe how you feel and how you react to them. Try to relax and let all the things that grab your attention pass away.

Inhale and then exhale—repeat this while you're seated there.

Step #6: Acknowledge your self-judgments and self-doubt

It is okay to have judgments—we all judge. And in fact, we even judge ourselves. But don't let your judgments about your failures or successes overwhelm you. Some of your self-judgments may even be so harsh to make you beat yourself up.

Sometimes self-doubt will also creep into your thoughts. You will judge yourself as unworthy, not worth it, undeserving, you can't do it, you're too weak, you don't have the willpower, or some other poorly assessed judgment of your character.

Don't do it. Don't allow judgments and self-doubt get the best of you.

Note that self-judgments are just like thoughts—they will come along, but then they will pass and fade away. They are not permanent. **Act like a quiet observer**. Listen to those self-judgments and then watch them fade away. Don't get caught up in them.

Step #7: Return to the Present

Now, this is the key here. All mindfulness exercises and all forms of mindfulness meditation will teach you that you need to redirect your attention back to the present. That in itself is at the core of being mindful that is being in the moment.

If your mind wanders, then forgive yourself and go back to focusing on what you are doing—trying to relax, inhaling, and exhaling.

If you begin to doubt yourself, then allow your doubts to fade, and then focus once more on your relaxed moment. Inhale and then exhale. Relax.

Do the same when a memory comes to mind. Acknowledge it and then allow it to fade. Finally, go back to the present. Breathe in and then breathe out.

Mindfulness Meditation Sample: Body Scan

The following is a simple mindfulness meditation exercise called the body scan. This is one of the first meditation exercises that you will usually be taught if you decide to get a meditation coach.

The body scan meditation will only take three to five minutes. Some people enjoy this exercise so much that they spend anywhere from 20 to 45 minutes. It's a great way to calm your mind and regain your focus.

You can do the body scan while sitting in your dedicated space for mindfulness practice, or you can do it while lying in bed. It's up to you which place you would like to do it.

Some mindfulness practitioners who can already do mindfulness exercises anywhere can do this exercise while sitting on the bus, while having a short coffee break at work, or while enjoying a nice afternoon sitting in the park.

But I would recommend that you do it in your dedicated space first. You will be applying most of the steps as it was described earlier for mindfulness exercises. For this meditation, I would suggest that you read the script below and record yourself.

You can record your voice using your phone as you sit in your special space. Once you're done recording, sit, relax, inhale/exhale slowly, and then hit play.

If you're ready, here's the script (no need to mention the numbers). Read slowly and don't rush:

1. Sit in a relaxed position.
2. Lie back until you feel comfy.
3. Close your eyes.
4. Take five deep breaths
5. Now, inhale slowly and deeply

6. Next, exhale slowly. emptying your lungs of all the air inside
7. Inhale deeply and slowly again
8. And then exhale deeply and slowly again
9. Repeat this slow and steady inhale and exhale pattern three more times
10. Keep repeating this breathing pattern until I tell you to open your eyes
11. Pay attention to how your feet are lying on the floor
12. Try to feel the weight of your feet as they press on the floor
13. Notice how your feet feel as they are pressed against the floor
14. Follow that sensation and then trace the sensations of your legs from your feet all the way to your knees
15. Notice how your knees feel
16. Bring your attention to your buttocks and the sensation that you feel as your bottom is pressed against the chair or bed
17. Breathe in and breathe out slowly
18. Feel the sensations that your hips are sending to your mind.
19. Trace the sensations going up your back all the way to your neck.

20. Notice the weight of your shoulders
21. Focus on the sensations that you feel in your arms as they gently lie on the surface of the chair or bed
22. Next, focus on the sensations being felt by your hands. Are your hands tense? Then release the tension in your hands.
23. Go back to your shoulders, neck, and throat. Notice how they feel.
24. Breathe in and breathe out. Relax.
25. Go up to your jaw and pay attention to how it feels. Is it tense? Then release the tension in your jaw. Relax. Breathe in and then breathe out.
26. Pay attention to the sensations that you are feeling on your face and head.
27. Do you feel any tension there as well? If there is any tension, then release and relax.
28. Breathe in and breathe out.
29. Count slowly from one to ten.
30. Now, open your eyes.

At the end of this exercise, you can go back to your regular breathing pattern. Let the feeling of calm and peace linger. You can even just sit in your chair or lie on the bed a minute or two more just to bask in the peace that you have just experienced.

Now, off you go to the rest of your day.

Chapter 4: More Actionable Tips to Build Self-Discipline

"Failure will never overtake me if my determination to succeed is strong enough."

(Og Mandino)

Do you need to reward yourself for becoming more motivated? When we try something new or try to form new habits, we are usually faced with discomfort. Sometimes we just want it to end, and so we throw in the towel and quit.

Is there a way to get rid of the discomfort of trying to obtain new habits? But maybe the discomfort is the key to your success, and you just didn't know it. In the previous chapter, we covered a lot of tips and tricks as well as habits that you can use to increase your level of self-discipline.

In this chapter, we will go over more of those tips that are also equally actionable. The topics we will discuss cover different facets of our lives. By doing so, we get a more well-rounded view of ultimately attaining self-discipline.

That One Simple Trick That Will Boost Your Motivation to Do Anything

Is it hard to stay motivated to do something? Yes, it is difficult. You wouldn't be reading all the way to this chapter if it was easy. Some might even say at this point is that what they thought they knew about motivation and self-discipline is wrong.

We have all been there—when we were excited about a new goal or habit that we want to achieve. We felt motivated, and we even believed that we could get it done. Maybe we made some progress along the way and that still kept us motivated.

But then we hit a proverbial wall.

There is a point when we can't keep moving forward. In short, there comes a point when we get stuck. So what do we usually do when discouragement gets in the way? We quit. And that's it.

Sometimes it all turns into a vicious cycle where we set a new goal, get excited and worked up about it, we try and fail, get some success, and then hit that wall again and then quit.

So, how do you get over that barrier? Why is there a barrier there in the first place? What's up with that wall?

Beating the Traditional Model for Motivation

There is a traditional model among researchers when it comes to our understanding of self-discipline and self-motivation. So what's the traditional model? Well, you're actually very familiar with it.

That model is the one that involves providing incentives to someone so that they will pursue a given course of action. It's like the carrot and stick method. You know how people used to make donkeys move forward? Tie a carrot at the end of a stick and hold that in front of a donkey (or some other animal), and it will keep chasing after the carrot.

Sometimes incentivizing works, but the magic of that method will have limits. Even the lure of an incentive or reward has its limits. Some researchers tweaked this model a little bit.

Self-Discipline Mastery

For instance, experts from the University of Pennsylvania say that how you deploy or provide the incentive can affect the recipient's motivation. This is from a study that they conducted [41].

That study suggests that people fear the loss of something more than we crave for rewards. The participants of that study were split into different groups. One group was promised to get a certain reward in dollars if they could make 7,000 steps each day.

They did the opposite with the other group. The researchers gave the monetary reward immediately to the test participants. But the deal was that the researchers would take away a certain amount from the money each time participants failed to reach the goal of 7,000 steps.

So who do you think were able to follow through with their commitment? If you guessed that it was the second group—the ones that were first given the reward—then you are right.

It would appear that the fear of losing the reward was bigger than any incentive of getting a reward.

That might sound useful in certain applications, but it isn't exactly the one that you will want to use when it comes to self-motivation.

The other limit to that approach is that it is still the carrot and stick method. Whether you give the reward in advance or you give the reward after, it is still the old model. And as time goes on, the lure of the reward or incentive will fail to motivate or even spark the interest of people.

Working with the Science behind Motivation

If you want to improve your motivation, then you must first understand the science behind it. Studies show that your brain tends to deplete its glucose stores every time you exert any form of self-control [42]. That includes times when you try so hard to stick to a goal, try a new habit, or even when you just try to push yourself to get things done.

However, in another study, students were observed as they underwent an adaptive learning program [43]. The study suggests that our ability to learn, remember, and stay motivated tends to increase over time.

Do we get tired due to continuous effort? The answer is yes. But we can stay motivated to continue if we use short, frequent bursts of activity instead of one continuous nonstop effort.

That One Simple Trick

Here's how you can use that scientific discovery to stay motivated to achieve a certain goal or obtain a new habit. This latest study shows that motivation and self-control doesn't decrease.

It's just that the brain just doesn't want to focus on that task that you have been doing for the last several hours or so. Your brain will want to maintain a balance and thus try to pull you away from that task so you can tend to other essential things as well—food, sleep, emotional support, etc., that you may already be neglecting due to continuous effort.

The same study suggests that after a minimum of 30 minutes performing the same task, your brain will want you to switch to something else. This has been identified as a kind of survival instinct.

The more you switch to different tasks, the better.

To hack this natural phenomenon, you should break down the new habit or task into several different chunks. Each of these sub-tasks should contribute to attaining the complete and original goal.

So let's say your goal or task is to complete a web page project. You can break it down into several sub-tasks such as:

- Article writing
- Page design
- Marketing
- Graphics
- Interactive features
- Social media features
- Videos

To stay motivated to finish the said task on time, what you should do is to assign 30 minutes for each of these tasks. You can do article writing for 30 minutes and then take a quick break.

But when you get back, switch your task to video content creation. After that, take another break, and when you get back, do some page design or marketing. If you vary your tasks from time to time, you can stay motivated and complete the entire project at the end of the day without feeling spent.

This same technique can be applied to habit-building and other goals that you might want to work on.

Move Towards Discomfort – How Discomfort Builds Character

You may have heard a preacher say at the pulpit or over the TV that pain and discomfort builds character. Well, don't worry. This next tip won't be so preachy. But there may be some golden nugget of truth to what pastors and preachers have been saying there.

Believe it or not, studies suggest that the more you live an easy and carefree life, the more it gets worse for you. The fact is that enduring tragedy and facing hardship is actually something good.

Discomfort, Pain, and Chaos Builds Character

Everyone endures pain and hardship at one time or another. It's part of the human experience. They bring about emotional upheavals but guess what—they can also bring about positive change.

We can come out of these difficult times with a newfound vision, greater strength, and better motivation. It is also a very basic human instinct to protect or shield ourselves from negative and painful experiences [44]. It's a survival instinct—you feel pain when you touch something, then you remember instinctively never to do it again.

You can also see this second hand when parents protect their children from getting hurt. Sometimes they can be overprotective and not allow their kids to run around or play on the playground.

However, getting your knee scraped or scratched during playtime is natural. It can even help a child learn and develop a lot faster. Children will encounter different attitudes while playing with other kids. You don't need to overshadow them all the time—allow them to experience varying attitudes, and some of those attitudes may even be offensive or perhaps even hurtful.

But expect your child to learn how to cope with difficult circumstances like that. It will become a life lesson that your child will learn.

A Paradigm Shift

What I'm asking you to do here is to go into a paradigm shift. Embrace discomfort and understand that it takes a little of that to increase your capacity to achieve and stay disciplined.

You can compare this idea to how our muscles work. If we don't use our muscles, atrophy will take over. Instead of growing strong, our muscles will grow weak and skinny. But if we use them during workouts, we'll get muscle pain. But that is how the muscle will grow—the growth happens after the pain.

Intermittent Fasting

You might be prompted to ask how intermittent fasting helps you become more disciplined. The answer is simple—it takes a lot of willpower to say no to food, especially when you're feeling hungry.

By choosing to fast and skip meals, you improve your self-mastery. You will become better able to resist the temptation of eating unhealthy food. This allows you to practice restraint and self-control, which you can apply in other decisions that you have to make.

Apart from that, intermittent fasting also brings you a lot of other benefits as well.

If you want to fast track healing and lose weight, then you should try intermittent fasting. Intermittent fasting is one of the trending ways people are losing weight today. However, it isn't easy. It is a health and fitness trend, and it is backed by actual science [45].

Intermittent fasting is not easy. It requires a lot of discipline and commitment. It will be difficult to practice during your first few weeks. You will feel the hunger pangs that will make you want to get something to eat. But if you learn to get over the initial challenge and strive for self-mastery, you will learn that you have better control over hunger and the temptation from sugary and unhealthy foods.

Do take note, however, that before you try it, you should first consult with your doctor. Some people who have certain conditions may be prohibited from trying this weight loss regimen.

Studies have shown that intermittent fasting has a lot of health benefits [46]. It may help people heal faster and live longer. But it may also be one of the most difficult habits that you will be doing in your life.

Intermittent Fasting: What It Is

Intermittent fasting is not a diet, but it is an eating pattern. In this eating pattern, you will have some fasting periods and also some eating periods as well. There are no specifications as to what food you're supposed to eat.

Again, remember that it is not a diet. There are different patterns or types of intermittent fasting too.

Intermittent fasting isn't new. Everyone goes on a fast every day. Why do you think we call the first meal of the day as "break-fast?" It literally means to end one's fast.

Let's say you have dinner at 7 pm and then go to bed. You then have breakfast at 7 am the following day. Guess what you just did? You had a 12-hour fast. You didn't eat anything.

Fasting is something incorporated within many religions too. But we're not going to push any form of religion here. We're just interested in this eating pattern.

Methods of Intermittent Fasting

I did mention that there are several types of intermittent fasting. We won't go into detail about them, but I will prescribe only the simplest and easiest methods in this list:

1. **The 5:2 Diet**: You are to consume only 500 to 600 calories on two days each week. That means you will fast for two days, but these are not two consecutive days.
2. **Eat Stop Eat Method**: This method will require you to go on a 24-hour fast. For instance, you will start fasting after dinner at 8 pm. The next meal that you will be

Self-Discipline Mastery

> having will be dinner the following day. This is a tough way to fast, I know.
>
> 3. **16/8 Method:** This method gives you only an eight-hour window to eat during your chosen fasting days. It can be noontime to 8 pm, 10 am to 6 pm, etc. Simply put, you fast for 16 hours and eat within the remaining eight hours, ergo 16/8.

Intermittent fasting drastically reduces your calorie intake, which, of course, has massive weight loss results. It isn't the easiest weight loss system to try and stick to.

I recommend the 16/8 method, and I do it twice each week. You don't need to go on an intermittent fast every day. It is the easiest of the three methods described above since you have a good enough amount of time to eat and get nourished.

Note that during your fasting days, you are allowed to drink water. It is not a total fast without food and drink.

Note that there are other intermittent fasting methods that I didn't mention here. There is also meal-skipping, alternate-day fasting, and then there is the warrior diet. For now, stick to the three that I described above, and I highly recommend that you try the 16/8 method if your doctor gives you the go signal.

*Remember to **check with your doctor first before you start fasting**.*

How to Stick to an Intermittent Fasting Regimen

Since intermittent fasting can be the toughest thing that you will be doing in your life to date, you will have to exercise a lot of discipline and self-control. The first few fasting days will be a test of your resolve and willpower. If you get over the first week, you will gain more self-control and discipline. Here are a few tips to help you stick with it.

- Eat nutrient-dense foods during fasting days. This includes foods that are rich in minerals, vitamins, and other nutrients as well. Eating those foods will help keep your blood sugar steady. You should eat a balanced diet during fasting days as much as possible.

- Season meals generously with herbs and spices. These food options are low in calories, but they help to enhance the flavor of your food.
- Eat high volume foods and food that has high water content such as melons, grapes, raw veggies, and popcorn.
- Eat more food that is rich in healthy fat, fiber, and protein. These are foods that are more filling and take longer to digest. They make you feel full longer, so you experience fewer hunger pangs.
- Avoid exercising or any other vigorous activity during your fasting days.
- Don't obsess about food during your fasting day. Don't read cookbooks and don't watch infomercials and cooking shows.
- Drink lots of water during your fasting days. You can also have herbal teas and other drinks too that are calorie-free.

Intermittent fasting teaches you to be more disciplined by saying no to food entirely on different occasions. When and how long you fast depends on the type of fasting regimen you want to employ. Through intermittent fasting, you regain control over your impulses and obtain more self-control. You become better able to resist the impulse to binge eat and become more disciplined about your food choices.

Cold Showers

Believe it or not, cold showers are quite beneficial to our health. It's not the most fun thing to do, but you can reap the benefits like:

- Improved metabolism
- Endorphins
- Improved blood circulation

What Are Cold Showers?

Cold showers are showers that you take where the water temperature is set to below 70°F. Now, that is cold, mind you. Experts refer to it as a type of hydrotherapy or water therapy.

The thing about it is that it isn't new. People have been doing cold showers for centuries and have noted the health benefits that they get out of it. The goal of the ancients who did cold showers was to condition their bodies; thus, they became more resistant to stress.

Benefits of Cold Showers Proven by Science

Research suggests that cold showers can help ease anxiety and depression [47]. This is because taking a cold shower can increase your endorphin and serotonin levels. These are the feel-good hormones. Increased endorphin and serotonin levels improve brain function, improve drive, increase mental energy, and help you to stay focused. With more mental energy and focus, you can stay disciplined throughout the day.

Studies also suggest that cold showers may be beneficial to weight loss [48]. This is due to the fact that taking a cold shower induces your body to produce more brown fat—the type of fat that is readily used by the body as energy. It's the first body fat to go and get burned as an energy source.

A lot of athletes today have incorporated cold showers into their training regimen [49]. They take advantage of the healing potential of cold showers and how it reduces inflammation, which is exactly what they are looking for during training.

Another study suggests that taking cold showers improves the way the body fights off common illnesses [50].

It's Not a Cure-All

Cold showers are not a cure-all, and they are not for everyone. If you are taking antidepressants or any mental health medication, then taking a cold shower may not be a good idea.

If your immune system has been compromised because you got sick rather recently, then you might want to forgo taking cold showers for now until you get better. On top of that, it will also take some effort to get used to taking cold showers.

How to Make the Cold Shower a Habit

Here are a few personal tips from me if you want to make taking a cold shower one of your lasting habits. Remember that it is not going to be easy, but it will be worth it.

1. **Don't rush, ease into it.** It will be very uncomfortable at first. So don't rush. If you can't take the cold any longer, then stop.
2. **Start with warm water and finish with warm water.** I would suggest that you start your shower with warm water. And then you slowly reduce the temperature until it goes below 70 degrees. Take a cold shower for a minute or two and then gradually increase the temperature until the water is warm enough for you. When you're used to it, you can do longer cold showers.
3. **Work your way to five minutes.** You can start by taking 30-second cold showers. Then work your way to one minute. After that, two. The goal is to work your way to a five-minute cold shower.

4. **Don't eat a heavy meal before a cold shower**. Eating heavy before a cold shower inhibits your body's blood flow. And it's not fun to have a belly full of food and then someone blasts you with really cold water.
5. **Start showering your face and neck.** That way, you won't feel the blast of cold water all over your body. This helps you get acclimated to the cold water.
6. **End your shower with something pleasurable**. I have always found that taking a hot cup of coffee or maybe chocolate can be quite a delight. Studies confirm that this method can help make it turn into an actual habit [51].

100 Days of Rejection Therapy

The story of Jiang Jia and his experience of getting 100 days of rejection is a classic example of how rejection can make you fearless. He resigned from a six-figure income working in a Fortune 100 company.

He quit that job because of an investment opportunity. But the plan backfired on him, and it left him with nothing.

He then discovered a game called Rejection Therapy. This game challenged people to look for rejections in their day-to-day lives. He tried it in the hopes that he would gain the ability to face rejections. He called it 100 days of rejection therapy.

Benefits of Rejection Therapy

1. **You will learn rejection-handling skills like flexing a muscle**: The more you get rejected, the less painful it becomes. You also get to work outside your comfort zone. The bottom line is that you get used to rejection; you don't take it personally, and it doesn't affect your mood.

2. **You will realize that it isn't really about you.** You no longer take rejection as something personal. People reject you because of their current circumstances at the moment, or maybe they were just not in the mood that day.

3. **You will learn to take risks**. Rejection therapy will teach you to take risks. Sometimes you will find the biggest opportunities after being rejected time and time again.

4. **You will learn how to turn a rejection into an opportunity**. Rejection is a painful experience; that is why a lot of us run away from it and then go into a corner and lick our wounds. Jiang says that rejections can have an upside and that if you can handle it well, you can find opportunities even while other people reject you.

There is no other way to get better at dealing with rejections than to find ways to get rejected. In my experience, it helped me get better at closing sales. I wasn't the best salesman—not by a long shot—but rejection therapy helped me learn how to close more sales eventually.

Here's what you can do. Make lots of requests every day and give people a chance to say no to your requests. Now, to reduce the pain of rejection, just remember that you're just trying to reach 100 rejections.

Turn everything into a countdown from 100 to zero. Be happy and celebrate when you reach 30 rejections, 50 rejections, 75 rejections, and finally 100 rejections. Write down your thoughts in a journal after experiencing each milestone on this list.

Building Routines

Gretchen Rubin once said: *"What you do every day matters more than what you do once in a while."* Your daily habits and routines, no matter how small they are, have a larger impact on your well-being than large, elaborate, and extravagant experiences.

Are you constantly looking for ways to make your days transition more smoothly? If you're anything like me, you will want to have more stability in your day. What I found out is that establishing routines helped me stay focused on what is important and allowed me to make time and space for my family.

That's one of the secrets to how I was able to maintain a healthy work-life balance.

Routines create consistency in everything that you do. They help you manage your time a lot better—well, you just put a lot of things on autopilot. You just have to deal with a few random things here and there.

Routines also encourage people to build habits and become more disciplined. However, if you're not careful, your routines can be more of a hindrance. This can happen if you're not mindful of it (remember the lesson in the previous chapter about mindfulness?).

In this chapter, we will go over a step-by-step plan so that you can create your routine mindfully and stick to it.

How a Routine Will Make You More Disciplined

I used to think that a routine was something that was beyond me. I was the type of person who preferred a degree of randomness in my day-to-day life. If I get too repetitive in the things I do, I lose focus and tend to become less productive.

Needless to say, I thought routines were mundane and boring. I also thought back then that I didn't have the gusto to follow through with any plan. I couldn't stick to an exercise plan, and I couldn't follow a lesson plan or an outline for a talk or presentation.

However, a few years going forward, routines have given me the stability I need to get creative. It has placed a lot of stability insomuch that I can creatively and efficiently do random things that can produce the best results—like writing this book, for instance.

One of the areas that I started with was my morning routine. It was a self-care habit that I have neglected for a while. But since learning how to make it a routine, I felt better and more empowered because my morning routine got me set up for the rest of my day.

Through routines, I was able to set up habits and add them to my routines. That helped me become more consistent in many aspects of my business. Having a routine allowed me to see that there is order in the things that I do—I learned I can be more organized!

As it was also mentioned elsewhere in this book, a routine will reduce the number of decisions that you will have to make on any given day. This is especially important on very busy days.

Downsides That You Should Know About

Do routines have downsides? It depends on the routine. Routines are like habits—there are bad habits and good habits. Just like that, there are bad routines and good routines.

Back in the day, I had this really bad routine. After coming home from work, I would just throw my keys on that little bowl on a cupboard where all the other keys in the house were in. And then the first thing I would do after kicking off my shoes was to go straight to the fridge and grab a drink.

The next step was to go to the couch and watch TV. The remote was somewhere on the couch—it was always there somewhere because I did this routine every day for about a year. I would sit there in front of the TV until I fell asleep.

That routine, of course, made me miserable. The house was unkempt, I gained weight, and I got depressed. That was an unhealthy nightly routine or after-work routine. I ended up isolating myself from my friends because I used the TV binging as a way to escape my troubles.

Some would argue that having a routine would stunt personal growth. And I agree—a bad routine will stunt your personal growth. But I also disagree because a good and mindfully selected routine will produce better personal growth.

A healthy routine has helped me get out of negative patterns. It also helped me prevent boredom from setting in, and I was able to get over burnouts.

How to Create a Healthy Mindful Routine

Here are the steps that I found were helpful when establishing a routine. Feel free to add to these steps in case you think you need to get something else done in between before moving on to the next step.

1. Choose the Type of Routine You Want to Have

This step is obvious. Some routines are for the mornings after you get out of bed, some can be done at night, and some during the midday.

Some routines are for work or, more specifically, to get you into work mode.

Some routines are for creative people. Artists may have their routine before they write songs, create music, or in my case, before I sit down to write a book. Athletes also have routines before practice and before going to work—aka the actual game.

Sometimes the best routine is the one that you have been doing all this time. In my case, I prepare a cup of coffee before I sit down in front of my laptop to write. I also set the early morning hours from 5 am to 7 am for writing.

I play my favorite playlist in the background too. That's my "get to work" music there.

And that is how I set my mind to get into work mode. Pay attention to the little things you do before you do something. Chances are you have the beginnings of an actual routine already there for you.

All you need, therefore, is to pick up on it and get started.

2. Set Your Motive

Now, you may want to set two to three minutes to do a mindfulness exercise when you're just starting out. You can do a body scan, or instead of a body scan, you can just do a mindfulness exercise to become more aware of your surroundings.

While you're at it, take that time to decide what you truly intend to do with this routine that you are about to engage in. Later on, after the routine has become more automatic, you can just skip this step if you want.

3. Start the Motions and Edit as You Go

After affixing your purpose and motive for that routine, then go for it. Start with full intent. Does it have to be a complex routine? Well, it's all up to you. I like to keep it simple so that I could get it done quickly.

But if you want to make it as elaborate as you want, then go ahead and do that. Whatever suits your fancy will work. Just make sure that you edit your routine to your needs and liking.

Try not to copy someone else's routine. Remember that these routines are personal, but if you think a part of another person's routine will help you stay focused and disciplined, then why not just incorporate that into your own routine, right?

4. Select Routines for Different Activities

You can have different routines for different activities in your day. Create a routine for different tasks so that they will become automatic to you.

Chapter 5: Dealing with Burnout the Smart Way

> *"Burnout is what happens when you try to avoid being human for too long."*
>
> *(Michael Gungor)*

Your ability to stay concentrated on a given task or goal will be negatively impacted if you are experiencing burnout. It will impede your progress when you're striving for self-mastery, and it will be very difficult to maintain a level of discipline.

If you are having problems coping with stress in the workplace, then you may be at risk of burnout. Burnouts can be quite challenging since they can leave you unable to cope with the demands of life.

I know, and I have been there. It affected my family life, and it definitely hit my work performance hard. I'm telling you, it's not just some random stuff that you come up with in your head. A burnout will feel as real as anything.

You feel empty and exhausted, and it may even be accompanied by physical and mental health symptoms too. But what is a burnout and how do you deal with it? You don't want it in your life, but at some point you will experience it and you will have to deal with it.

We'll cover the nature of a work burnout in this chapter. We will also go over some powerful tips and strategies that you can do to cope with it as well. A lot of the tips I will provide here has helped me get back up to my feet after having several burnout episodes in my life.

What is a Work Burnout Exactly?

According to the Mayo Clinic, job burnout is a special kind of work-related stress [52]. However, they also point out that it is not a medical diagnosis. What that means is that it isn't exactly a condition like depression.

It's not on the same level. But burnouts can still hit you hard. It affects people so much that experts recognize them as a type of occupational hazard [53]. The ones who are most susceptible to this experience are those in professions that require people-oriented contact.

If you're in human services, health care, customer service, or even in education, then you are highly susceptible to work burnouts. Any job description that requires a level of emotional and personal contact with others is included.

So, how do you define work burnout?

Burnout can be simply summarized in one word—exhaustion. This isn't like the regular exhaustion that you feel when you get tired after a hard day's work or after you went out for a run or lifted weights at the gym.

Three Types of Burnout

Experts have identified three different types of burnout syndrome. Dr. Christina Maslach, the one who formulated the Maslach Burnout Inventor, has identified them as the following:

1. Organizational Burnout

This is a type of burnout that is caused by poor organization. It can also come out of any extreme demands on your time. Another possible cause of this type of burnout is getting unrealistic deadlines at work.

Having these things will give you that feeling that your employment status is in jeopardy. Other than that, these conditions will also make you feel inadequate and that you aren't hitting your organization's goals all the time.

2. Interpersonal Burnout

This type of burnout is caused by getting into difficult relationships. This can happen in any of your relationships, both personally and professionally. If you are experiencing this, then a boss that is too aggressive can add to all the stress that you are already experiencing.

Having co-workers that intimidate or challenge you also adds fuel to the anxiety that you may already be experiencing. A spouse (or partner) that doesn't seem to appreciate you will make you feel unloved or unappreciated and may also contribute to interpersonal burnout.

3. Individual Burnout

This is a type of burnout that occurs on a personal level. A huge part of this type of burnout is the negative self-talk that people often do to themselves. Sometimes when you have set a rather perfectionist standard for yourself, it can also lead to this type of burnout.

Some people experience a certain level of neurosis when they experience an individual burnout. This can often lead people to a belief that all the things that they do can never be good enough even though they have already accomplished much.

Different Modes of Measuring Exhaustion and Burnout

Burnout is exhaustion that is physical, mental, and also emotional all at the same time. It is something that you will eventually go through after getting continual exposure to a lot of stressful situations.

Exhaustion from a researcher's point of view is measured differently, of course. When identifying the cause of burnout, you need to determine whether you're dealing with cognitive weariness, emotional exhaustion, or just physical fatigue [54]. That is the standard for the Shirom-Melamed Burnout Measure.

Another way that researchers measure the type of exhaustion that one may be experiencing is through making a distinction between psychological exhaustion and physical exhaustion [55], which is how the Copenhagen Burnout Inventory evaluates a person's condition.

Exhaustion also has a lot of other dimensions, and they are measured by other burnout measures/standards. Some experts check a person's enthusiasm in his or her job, levels of guilt, efficacy, adequacy in the workplace, and indolence.

These are all different measures, but they all boil down to one thing—when you're burned out, you are exhausted in more ways than one. Because burnouts are heavily caused by stress, psychiatrists Gail North and Herbert Freudenberger have classified burnouts as a type of stress syndrome.

A Short History about the Concept of a Burnout

Long story short, a burnout zaps out the joy in your life, and it will haunt your family and personal interactions, your friendships, and it can have a negative influence on your career. It happens after working long hours, getting upsetting news, having a sick family member, school or work safety issues, and other possible causes.

We'll go over the causes later on.

The word "burnout" was coined in the 1970s by Herbert Freudenberger [56]. He described it as a condition that involves a severe amount of stress. This highly stressful and prolonged condition then leads to an equally severe emotional, mental, and physical exhaustion.

If you have experienced burnout, you know that it is a lot worse than any regular kind of fatigue. If you're going through one, you will find it challenging to deal with your day-to-day responsibilities.

Your productivity will hit rock bottom. Your relationships with loved ones and friends will suffer. On top of that, you will find it increasingly more difficult to deal with the stress that happens in life.

Who Can Get Affected by Burnouts

Have you ever felt like you have nothing left to give? Have you ever experienced feeling that fear of leaving your bed and you just don't want to get up in the morning when your alarm rings?

That may be a sign of burnout coming along. It will come with a feeling of hopelessness, and then you develop a rather pessimistic outlook in life. Now, here's the scary part—a burnout never goes away on its own, and it can affect anybody.

If it is left untreated, it will lead to other medical conditions. It can develop into depression, and it can also contribute to diabetes and even heart disease.

As it was pointed out earlier, some people are more susceptible to burnouts. Here's a partial list:

- Parents

- Business executives
- Doctors
- Nurses
- Any first responders to emergency situations
- Customer service representatives
- Technicians
- Cab drivers
- Waitresses
- Construction workers
- Office staff
- Front desk staff
- Any professional that is tasked with helping others

As you can see, any job that requires any form of direct interaction and providing service to others is a trigger for this type of condition. One study even suggests that you don't have to be at the forefront of emergency care to rapidly experience a burnout.

Even being a father or a mother caring for a child can put you at risk for burnouts. In fact, parents, business executives, and even doctors are on the same level of potential risk for this condition [57].

Note that you don't have to be a kind of service personnel to experience burnout. Anyone can experience it given certain conditions. We'll cover the contributory conditions and factors in a later section of this chapter.

Be Aware of the Burnout Signs: Some Important Q&A

The following are the signs and symptoms of burnout. If you experience two or more of these signs, then you know that you are at risk of one coming up real soon. Take some alone time and ask yourself the following questions:

- Am I experiencing bowel problems, stomach aches or other stomach problems, unexplained headaches, and other physical symptoms?
- Have I experienced changes in my sleeping habits?
- Do I use alcohol, drugs, or even food just to make me feel better? Do I use any of

these things just to feel numb about the things happening in my life?
- Am I experiencing any form of disillusionment from my current job?
- Do I feel dissatisfied with the achievements that I have had at work?
- Do I find it hard to concentrate?
- Do I lack the energy to be productive as consistently as I used to?
- Am I irritable when interacting with clients, customers, and even with my co-workers?
- Do I have trouble getting work started?
- Do I have to drag myself to work all the time?
- Have I become critical of my workmates or even my superiors?
- Have I become more cynical nowadays?

If you answered in the affirmative to two or more of these questions, then you have the definite symptoms of burnout.

In my case, I only noticed that I was having a burnout when my sleeping patterns changed. I often try to stay up late at night rushing to complete a project, only to fall asleep on my desk and struggle to stay up.

I ended up sleeping two to three hours a day. I then felt dissatisfied with my work—it's work that I have been very good at, and I've been doing it for more than five years. I was snapping at my family and I couldn't stand my co-workers.

If you are experiencing burnout, I strongly suggest that you talk to your doctor immediately. And I do mean immediately. You may get a referral to work with a psychiatrist or some other mental health provider, especially if your doctor suspects that your burnout may be related to depression.

List of Psychological Symptoms You May Experience

- Frustration
- Emotional numbness
- Cynicism
- Easily angered
- Absenteeism
- Loss of purpose

- Low commitment to one's job role
- Negative attitude towards co-workers
- Fatigue
- Lack of creativity
- Difficulty concentrating
- Low mood
- Feeling listless
- Detachment
- Anxiety
- Generalized aches
- Feeling really exhausted

List of Physical Symptoms You May Experience

- Muscle tension
- Susceptibility to flu, colds, and other common ailments
- Difficulty sleeping
- Disrupted sleep cycle
- Hypertension
- Gastrointestinal disorders
- Headache

Now, we'll go over the more serious symptoms in the next section of this discussion. We'll cover that below.

Key Symptoms That You Should Look Out For

Here are the key symptoms that can help you identify whether you're already experiencing burnout or not:

1. Exhaustion

This is usually one of the early signs that you will experience. When we say exhaustion, this is the kind that leaves you completely depleted. It's not just an emotional or mental kind of exhaustion—this one is accompanied by actual physical symptoms.

Other than feeling tired and unmotivated without much gusto to carry on any further, you also experience certain aches and pains. You will get a loss of appetite. I have experienced stomach aches for no reason. I also had frequent headaches.

2. Frequent Illnesses

Okay, so this is a separate symptom altogether from the ones mentioned in item number 1 above. Remember that burnout is often related to long-term exposure to stress. When that happens, your immune system suffers.

The body becomes weak and eventually susceptible to many common illnesses. If you're under constant stress for a prolonged period of time, then you will usually get flu-like symptoms, cough, cold, and other health conditions as well.

Since you will already experience some changes in your sleep patterns, you may already be going through the first few stages of insomnia. As your condition progresses, you may develop anxiety disorders as well as depression as well.

3. Irritability

Here's a fact—burnouts can cause you to lose control. As the level of your anxiety increases, the more you become irritable. You lose your cool with your kids, your spouse or partner, and your co-workers as well.

You get easily irritated and you lash back at people quite easily. You weren't always that way, but now you have become a hot-headed person.

You can't tolerate a lot of things and you tend to snap at other people over the smallest things.

As you go along, you find it more difficult to cope with the usual stressors in life, such as household tasks, caring for your kids, and even work meetings. When something goes wrong or some unplanned thing happens, you get irritated.

4. Escape Fantasies

People experiencing burnout will usually fantasize about going on a solo vacation or running away from their current situation in general. There are also extreme circumstances when they may turn to substance abuse to just numb away any pain they may be experiencing.

5. Isolation

When you are overwhelmed, you will feel isolated. Sometimes this isolation is self-imposed. Burned out people may stay away from people or just stop any form of socializing completely.

They stop confiding with friends and family. This is a critical sign, and when you notice it happening to you, then you must get help immediately.

Causes of Burnouts

It is important that when you notice that you have a burnout that you determine the possible causes with your healthcare provider. The following are some of the factors that can lead to work burnout:

- ***Lack of Work-Life Balance***

When your work takes up a lot of your time, then you are on the verge of a burnout. Remember that human beings aren't one-dimensional creatures. Our life at work is only one facet of the totality of our being.

We all need to have time for something else and other people. We need to spend enough time and energy for our family, friends, and other interests. Lack of work-life balance can easily lead to burnout.

- ***Lack of Social Support***

Feeling isolated at work is a dangerous thing. Combine that with isolation and loneliness in your personal life can add to the stress that you are already feeling. You need to reach out and find friends pretty much everywhere.

Remember that it is not the isolation that gets you. It is the stress that comes from a lonely life that will contribute to your stress levels.

- ***Extremely Monotonous Activity***

Last time I checked, you're not a machine. Look at yourself in the mirror and you will see that on the other side is a human being. You're not built to do the same thing over and over again. It's going to drive you into boredom or even chaos.

I find it very hard to remain focused if I keep repeating the same things over and over again ad infinitum at work. The first thing that will come is fatigue. You get tired of doing the same routine.

It will eventually lead to burnout. That means we should find time to break the monotony of our lives in order to derive more meaning into what we do for a living.

- ***Problematic Workplace Dynamics***

I never encountered any office bullies in my life, but I have been bullied at school, so I guess I know how it would feel like. But there have been people in the office that have undermined my work, and that felt almost like I was getting bullied.

I have also had a boss micromanage everything, and that can also contribute to dysfunctional workplace dynamics.

- **_Unclear Job Expectations_**

When the degree of authority that you are given (or someone who is supposed to be your superior is given), then you will feel uncomfortable at work. You won't know what is appropriate and what is expected of you or your co-workers performance-wise.

- **_Lack of Control_**

When you feel like you have no control over your tasks, or your ability to influence certain decisions, then that might trigger feelings of insecurity.

Having no control over things like your workload, your work schedule, the assignments that you have to work on, and the unavailability of the resources that you need to fulfill your job can produce a lot of anxiety and thus contribute a lot to a possible burnout.

Burnout Prevention

Once you have identified one or two of the symptoms mentioned earlier, you should act promptly. Here are some of the expert tips that I have found useful when it comes to burnout prevention.

Increase Self-Efficacy

"Self-efficacy" is a technical term, and it simply means having that firm belief that you can accomplish things.

Experts also call it a "perceived capability"[59]. When you set these goals, they should be ones that are meaningful to you.

Experts have observed that the people who believe that they can achieve things tend to experience less stress. When people believe that they can overcome problems, then they find inner strength to overcome stressful situations.

According to Albert Bandura, the one who formulated this theory, there are four sources that drive this firm belief in oneself. They include the following:

1. Mastery experiences
2. Verbal persuasion
3. Psychological and emotional states
4. Vicarious experiences

You can use these factors to improve your state or level of self-efficacy.

Mastery Experiences

So, what are mastery experiences? A mastery experience is an experience where you take on a new challenge and then you succeed in it. This can be applied when learning a new skill or achieving a certain goal.

We improve our performance one step at a time, and we gain increased confidence as we master small steps toward a much larger goal. So, how do you do this?

1. Find a task that you find challenging (e.g., increasing sales, creating a marketing strategy, ask someone out on a date, complete your research on a given deadline, etc.)

2. Outline smaller tasks that will help you complete that task (e.g., design ads, send a text message, engage in small talk, etc.)
3. Do one small task at a time until you have accomplished every single one of them. Observe how you feel after accomplishing each task. Know that you can do it if you try.
4. After successfully accomplishing a task, perform a self-evaluation session. Find some quiet time—maybe 10 to 15 minutes—take the time to celebrate what you have accomplished. You can get a drink or maybe have a favorite dessert; any treat will be great. And then while you're at it ask yourself, "I can do this, so what else can I do?"
5. Move on to the next mini-task until you have accomplished the main task. Don't forget to reward yourself at the end.

So, what if you encounter failure? The solution is to sit down and also do a self-evaluation. This time you will determine the factors that brought about your failure. Think about things that you would have done differently.

After that, determine your next course of action or an alternative action. And then go out and do it.

Vicarious Experiences

This is the second most powerful way to increase your self-efficacy. The word "vicarious" sort of sounds quite religious, but it means something very simple. What this means is that you should observe someone else who has already accomplished that thing you want to accomplish.

What you are looking for is someone to "model" how the task can be accomplished. For instance, if you don't feel confident about selling (you believe yourself to be a bad salesperson), then find someone good at it.

Observe how it is done. Bandura says that seeing someone succeed is rather infectious. If they can do it, then that means you can do it as well.

The person who will serve as your model doesn't have to be a co-worker, supervisor, or even your boss. It can be a grandparent, your siblings, an aunt, teachers, your coach, a local celebrity, or any mentor.

What matters is that you can vicariously envision yourself as succeeding using the method that they used to succeed.

Verbal Persuasion

There are some big reasons why people look for motivational speakers. People attend self-improvement seminars and mastery classes conducted by charismatic experts for a reason.

Motivational talks and even that little pep talk that you have with a close friend can help to raise your spirits and reduce stress. It has the same effect as a talk between a parent and a child. That trust and confidence communicated from a trusted person (e.g., the parent) provides solace and motivation for the recipient (e.g., the child).

Psychological and Emotional States

Your emotional state and psychological condition can also be a source of strength and provide you a big boost to one's self-efficacy. It should be obvious that you can't have a positive assessment of your own capability to accomplish anything if you're suffering from depression and/or anxiety.

It won't be realistic to presume that you can get your tasks done if you are currently suffering from a medical condition. A lot of times, when people get over poor psychological and emotional states, they bounce back and take on life with much-needed gusto. They see things as a new chance at life.

Chapter 6 – Discipline Tactics of Navy SEALs and the Spartans

A lot of soldiers and former service members have written entire books on how the Navy SEALs, the Spartans, or other figures that enforce discipline among their numbers. Examples of such authors include Mark Grant, former SEAL Jocko Willink, and Jason Lopez. This chapter goes over ideas and insights that these authors and others like them have shared.

Success = Discipline

Discipline is a necessity, especially when your life is on the line. Self-discipline is on the same level of importance as mental toughness, resilience, and hard work when the safety and fate of a nation is in your hands.

Well, you don't have to enter into military service in order to learn about their methods. You can learn from these authors themselves and pick up lessons from their personal experiences.

When you're a soldier, you embrace pain and hardship as if they were your life and joy. You try to excel and do your best because you know that if you fail hundreds, if not thousands, of lives are at stake.

Military Secrets

Here are some of the rules of thumb and guiding principles that the Navy SEALs and other military service members live by in order to maintain self-control, willpower, and self-discipline.

Don't Quit

Don't quit? Easier said than done, right? This is more of a motto for service members. When faced with challenges, they don't quit. They look at the challenge and act as if they have no other choice but to go forward.

Next time you are faced with seemingly insurmountable odds, think back on the SEALs and how they sacrifice and push forward despite difficulty and pain. Sometimes it takes sheer persistence and determination to see things through.

Always Make Every Goal and Objective a Serious Thing

If you go into the field half-cocked or if you try something and the will is half-baked, then you're bound to fail. According to former Navy SEAL Casey Imafidon, SEALs emphasize only three things when it comes to missions:

1. The objective
2. How to execute it
3. What happens after you have reached that objective

He says that sometimes your success is measured by the level of commitment you give to a specific goal or objective.

Wake Up Early and Win the Morning

We have discussed waking up early in an earlier chapter of this book. There is a reason why military service members are made to wake up early as a matter of routine. Waking up early doesn't only instill a feeling of discipline; it also gives you a lot of opportunities such as:

- Complete all the necessary preparations for that day
- Read a book and prepare your mind
- Meditate
- Exercise
- Gather the necessary intel
- Start your day with better focus and discipline

Jocko Willink also created what he called the 4 AM Club. This is support and a collaboration of a group of people who wake up at 4 in the morning, plan their day well ahead of everyone else, and be better at achieving their goals.

Other than waking up early in the morning, another accompanying or complementing principle that Navy Seals have is called winning the morning.

For military service members, the choice you make every morning is only a simple matter. When the alarm goes off, you have a critical decision to make—do you get up and get your day started, or do you succumb to the comfort of your bed and go back to sleep?

Those who choose to snooze eventually lose, but those who choose to get up win. This simple exercise allows you to overcome a moment of weakness. Overcoming weaknesses eventually become a powerful habit.

Pay Attention to Every Lesson That You Learn

Both the successes and failures that you experience will become your mentors. In many instances, your failures tend to become your biggest and loudest teachers. Navy SEALs are taught leadership principles, and that includes making course corrections quickly.

A quick lesson here is that you shouldn't dwell too much on your failures because it will do nothing for you. Adapt quickly and make adjustments as fast as you can when failure strikes. When there's a lot at stake, there's no time to mull over spilled milk.

Exercise

All soldiers are forced to exercise daily. We all know that there are numerous studies on the benefits of exercise, so there is no need to enumerate every single one of them. One of the most notable benefits of pushing yourself to exercise is that, according to studies, it can increase your emotional and mental resilience [62].

Embrace the Suck

This is military slang that was coined during Operation Iraqi Freedom. So what does it mean? The lesson is powerful here. It implies that you're not the first one to ever experience difficulty and pain, so deal with it. But remember you're not doing it alone.

To embrace the suck means to embrace the situation—to accept that you are really in the current situation you're in. However, that is not a defeatist notion. Sure, you accept the reality of the conditions you're living in now, but you have the power to do something about it.

As soldiers, the Navy Seals have no choice but to go where they are told to go. They do not deny the challenges that they face. This reduces any feelings of discontent among service members.

So, why does the military, including the Spartans, "embrace the suck?" The answer is simple—they do it because it is now a matter of habit. When you rewire your mind and take a more accepting point of view, you will become more aware of your situation and thus will be more likely to spot opportunities to come out victorious.

Mastering the Art of Simplicity

Navy Seals and other military personnel often get told to "cut the crap." It's more than just another military slang or wisecrack. Mark Divine, a former Navy Seal, explains that this principle refers to the art of simplicity.

He says that in order to live with more grit and discipline, we need to learn to live and embrace the art of simplicity. It is quite a liberating concept. We often clutter our lives with lots of gadgets, commitments, unhealthy relationships, and way too many material possessions.

These are things that weigh us down and take away our focus on the things that matter. In effect, the "crap" in our lives distracts us and reduces our effectiveness. We become less disciplined in everything we do because we think of and pay attention to too many things.

In the military, service members live and breathe simplicity. They are given an objective and then they set out to complete the mission and attain the aforementioned objective.

To a soldier, war is nothing but chaos. And so, an objective, a mission, and cutting out the unnecessary things that are in the way help to get rid of the chaos.

Do you want to be more disciplined? Here's what you can do:

1. Decide today to live a simpler life—try a minimalist lifestyle.
2. If you have too many clothes and many of which you never even wear anymore, then get rid of those or give them away to charity.

3. Make an inventory of each room in the house.
4. Start with your bedroom. Find things in there that are just gathering dust, things that you haven't used in the last six to twelve months.
5. Get rid of those or give them away to charity (another option is to collect these items and have a garage sale so you can make some money on the side).
6. Next, go to the living room. Do the same inventory.
7. Make an inventory of every place in your house—especially the garage and your attic. You might be surprised to find that you have been hoarding a lot of stuff that you don't need or use.
8. Clean up these living spaces and put the unused items on sale or give them away to charity (at least you know you're helping other people in the process).
9. Check the emails that you receive. Cancel subscriptions that you don't read or use.
10. Are there people in your life who are nuisances or distractions to you? You have the choice to either put them on your

ignore list or just cut ties with them completely. How you do that is all up to you.
11. Are there gym memberships and other subscriptions that you're paying for that you don't really need or rarely use? Get rid of those as well.
12. Is social media taking up too much of your time? You should try uninstalling some of your phone's social media apps.

If you do these things, you live simply and will be adopting a minimalist lifestyle. You will then notice a sense of freedom and clarity, especially after you have removed all the clutter in your home and in your life.

It will be as if you have been renewed. You can now approach your days with better focus and renewed commitment to the things that really matter to you.

In Mark Divine's own words—in the eyes of the Navy Seals, less means more.

You're Never Really Alone

Admiral William McRaven once said that no one wins wars alone. The same is true when we want to win the war against the lack of focus and self-discipline. To have mental toughness, you need to realize that you're not the only one trying to achieve that character trait.

This lesson is usually driven home hard into every Navy Seal. Remember, they are called Navy Seal Teams—there is no room for a one-person army like Rambo or some other fictional war character.

All you need to do is to observe their physical trainings. You will notice that a lot of these trainings involve a degree of strategic teamwork. It's not just teamwork—you're part of a greater whole, and you need to contribute to the strategy that your team will implement to ensure that the mission is a success.

When one person makes a mistake, the entire class gets the brunt of it. However, they're not just on a mission to weed out the weak. The goal is to teach new recruits a lesson. And that lesson is that teamwork is essential to success.

Navy Seals understand this lesson early in training. They understand that they must act as an entire unit and not just individually. That works in military life as well as in life outside of the service.

Here's what you can do:
1. Find support in every endeavor. You can find support groups, clubs, and other organizations. Share your own experiences and be immersed in the experiences of others.
2. The goal is to find likeminded individuals who are willing to encourage you.
3. Find someone, a spouse, a dear friend, a life coach, a therapist, etc. with whom you can confide in. Have regular performance evaluations with that person, whether it is about being more disciplined, gaining more self-control, earning more money, anger management, etc. The goal is to have someone to whom you can report your progress to. Remember that when effort is measured, then progress

increases, and when it is reported and evaluated, then progress multiplies.

4. Reach out to someone and do some good in that person's life. You can volunteer in a soup kitchen or some other cause. This also gets reported back to your friend or confidant. Remember that when people join an endeavor that is something bigger than themselves, their performance tends to increase.

Marianna Pogosyan, a consultant that specializes in cross-cultural transition psychology, and author of the book *Between Cultures,* explains that when people get involved in helping others, they eventually help themselves.

Being in the service of others produces altruistic feelings, but it is more than just that. Studies show that when we go out of our way to help others, it improves our emotional well-being. It improves our ability to empathize with others and increases our capacity to cope with stress.

Our performance and self-control also increase when we focus on tasks that benefit others. Why are Navy Seals more dedicated and more disciplined compared to a lot of people? It is because they understand that what they are doing benefits others.

When the lives of others are at stake, you push yourself to greater heights. Sometimes you find that you can do things better because of this. It eventually gives you a sense of purpose and satisfaction that you can't get anywhere else. It is an act that naturally cycles back to benefit you in the end.

You Need to Challenge Yourself Constantly

Former Navy Seal Cade Courtley explains that you should expect that "you're going to get your ass kicked once in a while" and that is why you should make it a point to constantly challenge yourself.

He says that there is a common factor that is shared by all who succeed at BUDs training. BUDs is short for Basic Underwater Demolition SEAL training. It is a physical and mental training that all candidates go through before they ultimately become part of the Navy Seals.

Courtley explains that this single factor is finding a reason to continue to grow and improve. Challenge yourself constantly and learn to live with true adversity. He observes that the candidates who survive BUDs are those who have lived and survived against adversity their entire lives.

He then makes an interesting analogy. He asks, "Who will you be more prone to trust—someone who inherited millions of dollars or someone who built his financial empire of 10 million dollars at age 45 after going through several bankruptcies to get there?

The more resilient and more disciplined person whom you should emulate is the person who has made all the mistakes and has thrived in adversity. Find a way to challenge yourself, and you will learn to thrive in the same manner.

Did you get promoted a couple of years ago? Did you stop there, and did the drive and ambition die out after you got your pay raise? Challenge yourself to perform better and you will find yourself in a lot of adversity, but that challenge will drive you forward and give you the mental toughness to face even greater difficulties ahead.

Were you able to lose ten pounds in the last two months? But are you at your target weight? If not, then challenge yourself to lose ten more pounds. This will help you become even more disciplined with your workout and stick with your diet plan.

The greater the challenge, the more self-control, grit, and discipline will be required. Beat that, and you will achieve greater levels of self-mastery.

Conclusion

I hope that the lessons here in this book were able to help you understand the logic and science behind self-discipline, motivation, and willpower. It will take a while for practices and lessons like developing and shifting to a new mindset to completely set in.

In your journey to self-mastery, you will be faced with fear, uncertainty, and doubt. I suggest that you try out the habits that have been outlined here from delayed gratification to mindfulness.

Don't stress so much about the outcome, but please learn to enjoy the process. It is not just the end result that brings joy and satisfaction to the soul—the journey itself is something that you should look forward to.

The next step is to practice the principles in this book and get an accountability partner. Find someone who will walk the path to a more self-disciplined life with you. It is never easy, but just like the Spartans of old and the Navy SEALs of today, every task and journey is made easier when you have someone to share it with.

Thank you!

Before you go, I just wanted to say thank you for purchasing my book.

You could have picked from dozens of other books on the same topic but you took a chance and chose this one.

So, a HUGE thanks to you for getting this book and for reading all the way to the end.

Now I wanted to ask you for a small favor. **Could you please consider posting a review on the platform? Reviews are one of the easiest ways to support the work of independent authors.**

This feedback will help me continue to write the type of books that will help you get the results you want. So if you enjoyed it, please let me know! (-:

Lastly, don't forget to grab a copy of your Free Bonus book *"Bulletproof Confidence Checklist."* If you want to learn how to overcome shyness and social anxiety and become more confident, then this book is for you.

Resource Page

1 Duckworth, A.L. (2011, February 15). The significance of self-control.
https://www.ncbi.nlm.nih.gov/pmc/articles/PMC3041117/

2 Englert, C. (2016, March 2). The Strength Model of Self-Control in Sport and Exercise Psychology.
https://www.ncbi.nlm.nih.gov/pmc/articles/PMC4773600/

3 Muraven, M. (2010, March 1). Building Self-Control Strength: Practicing Self-Control Leads to Improved Self-Control Performance.
https://www.ncbi.nlm.nih.gov/pmc/articles/PMC2855143/

4 Pychyl, T.A. (2010, January 21). Implementation Intentions Facilitate Action Control.
https://www.psychologytoday.com/us/blog/dont-delay/201001/implementation-intentions-facilitate-action-control

5 Steakley, L. (2011, December 29). The science of willpower.

http://scopeblog.stanford.edu/2011/12/29/a-conversation-about-the-science-of-willpower/

6 Gailliot, M.T. & Baumeister, R.F. (2007, November). The physiology of willpower: linking blood glucose to self-control. https://www.ncbi.nlm.nih.gov/pubmed/18453466

7 Lenz, M. (2016, October 20). 3 TIPS FOR BUILDING SUCCESSFUL HABITS. https://due.com/blog/3-tips-building-successful-habits/

8 Klein, G. (2016, May 1). Mindsets: What they are and why they matter. https://www.psychologytoday.com/us/blog/seeing-what-others-dont/201605/mindsets

9 Lally, P., Van Jaarsveld, C.H.M., Potts, H.W.W., & Wardle, J. (2009, July 16). How are habits formed: Modelling habit formation in the real world. http://citeseerx.ist.psu.edu/viewdoc/download?doi=10.1.1.695.830&rep=rep1&type=pdf

10 Rehman; I., Mahabadi; N., & Rehman, C.I. (2019, June 18). Classical Conditioning.

https://www.ncbi.nlm.nih.gov/books/NBK470326/

11 Nelis, S.M., Thom, J.M., Jones, I.R., Hindle, J.V., & Clare, L. (2018, January 8). Goal-setting to Promote a Healthier Lifestyle in Later Life: Qualitative Evaluation of the AgeWell Trial. https://www.ncbi.nlm.nih.gov/pmc/articles/PMC5942145/

12 Barry, N. (2012, October 24). The commitment that changed my career + my next project. https://nathanbarry.com/commitment-changed-career/

13 Lally, P., Wardle, J., & Gardner, B. (2011, August). Experiences of habit formation: a qualitative study. https://www.ncbi.nlm.nih.gov/pubmed/21749245

14 Oettingen, G. & Mayer, D. (2002, November). The motivating function of thinking about the future: expectations versus fantasies. http://www.ncbi.nlm.nih.gov/pubmed/12416922

15 Pham, L.B. & Taylor, S.E. (1999, February 1). From Thought to Action: Effects of Process-

Versus Outcome-Based Mental Simulations on Performance. https://journals.sagepub.com/doi/abs/10.1177/0146167299025002010

16 Baumeister, R. F., Bratslavsky, E., Muraven, M., & Tice, D.M. (1998). Ego depletion: Is the active self a limited resource? http://psycnet.apa.org/journals/psp/74/5/1252/

17 Pozen, R.C. (2012, September 19). MANAGING YOURSELF: Boring Is Productive. http://blogs.hbr.org/hbsfaculty/2012/09/boring-is-productive.html

18 Twito, L., Israel, S., Simonson, I., & Knafo-Noam, A. (2019, July 31). The Motivational Aspect of Children's Delayed Gratification: Values and Decision Making in Middle Childhood. https://www.ncbi.nlm.nih.gov/pmc/articles/PMC6684787/

19 Mischel, W., Shoda, Y., & Rodriguez, M.I. (1989, May 26). Delay of gratification in children.

https://www.ncbi.nlm.nih.gov/pubmed/2658056

20 Mischel, W., Shoda, Y., & Peake, P.K. (1988, April). The nature of adolescent competencies predicted by preschool delay of gratification. https://www.ncbi.nlm.nih.gov/pubmed/3367285

21 Shoda, Y., Mischel, W., & Peake, P.K. (1990, November). Predicting Adolescent Cognitive and Self-Regulatory Competencies From Preschool Delay of Gratification: Identifying Diagnostic Conditions. https://www.researchgate.net/publication/232585605_Predicting_Adolescent_Cognitive_and_Self-Regulatory_Competencies_From_Preschool_Delay_of_Gratification_Identifying_Diagnostic_Conditions

22 Kidd, C., Palmeri, H., & Aslin, R.N. (2013, January). Rational snacking: young children's decision-making on the marshmallow task is moderated by beliefs about environmental reliability. https://www.ncbi.nlm.nih.gov/pubmed/23063236

23 Carroll, N. (2013, November 3). STURGEON'S LAW: WHAT DOES IT HAVE TO DO WITH YOU?
https://nancycarroll.net/sturgeons-law

24 Harvey, H.B. & Sotardi, S.T. (2018, June). The Pareto Principle.
https://www.ncbi.nlm.nih.gov/pubmed/29706287

25 Lally, P., van Jaarsveld, C.H.M., Potts, H.W.W., & Wardle, J. (2009, July 16). How are habits formed: Modelling habit formation in the real world.
https://onlinelibrary.wiley.com/doi/abs/10.1002/ejsp.674

26 Dalle, G.R., Calugi, S., Molinari, E., Petroni, M.L., Bondi, M., Compare, A., Marchesini, G.; & QUOVADIS Study Group. (2005, November). Weight loss expectations in obese patients and treatment attrition: an observational multicenter study.
https://www.ncbi.nlm.nih.gov/pubmed/16339128

27 King, A.C., Castro, C.M., Buman, M.P., Hekler, E.B., Urizar, G.G. Jr., & Ahn, D.K.

(2013, October). Behavioral impacts of sequentially versus simultaneously delivered dietary plus physical activity interventions: the CALM trial. https://www.ncbi.nlm.nih.gov/pubmed/23609341

28 Meinert, L., Kehlet, U., & Aaslyng, M.D. (2012, October). Consuming pork proteins at breakfast reduces the feeling of hunger before lunch. https://www.ncbi.nlm.nih.gov/pubmed/22554612

29 Rains, T.M., Leidy, H.J., Sanoshy, K.D., Lawless, A.L., & Maki, K.C. (2015, February 10). A randomized, controlled, crossover trial to assess the acute appetitive and metabolic effects of sausage and egg-based convenience breakfast meals in overweight premenopausal women. https://www.ncbi.nlm.nih.gov/pubmed/25889354

30 Larun, L., Brurberg, K.G., Odgaard-Jensen, J., & Price, J.R. (2015, February 10). Exercise therapy for chronic fatigue syndrome. https://www.cochranelibrary.com/cdsr/doi/10.1002/14651858.CD003200.pub3/full

31 Gardner, J.M. (2020, January 11). Personal productivity and the two-career household: The AIR method. https://www.ncbi.nlm.nih.gov/pmc/articles/PMC6997848/

32 Tracy, B. (n.d.) Eat That Frog: Brian Tracy Explains The Truth About Frogs. https://www.briantracy.com/blog/time-management/the-truth-about-frogs/

33 Supersoul, Season 6, Episode 608. (2015, April 12). Is There a Difference Between Mindfulness and Meditation? http://www.oprah.com/own-super-soul-sunday/is-there-a-difference-between-mindfulness-and-meditation-video

34 Keng, S.L., Smoski, M.J., & Robinsa, C.J. (2011, May 13). Effects of Mindfulness on Psychological Health: A Review of Empirical Studies. https://www.ncbi.nlm.nih.gov/pmc/articles/PMC3679190/

35 Chambers, R., Lo, B.C.Y., & Allen, N.B. (2007, February 23). The Impact of Intensive Mindfulness Training on Attentional Control,

Cognitive Style, and Affect. https://rd.springer.com/article/10.1007/s1060 8-007-9119-0

36 Ireland, T. (2014, June 12). What Does Mindfulness Meditation Do to Your Brain? https://blogs.scientificamerican.com/guest-blog/what-does-mindfulness-meditation-do-to-your-brain/

37 Research on Mindfulness. (n.d.) https://www.mindfulschools.org/about-mindfulness/research-on-mindfulness/

38 Lazar, S.W., Kerr, C.E., Wasserman, R.H., Gray, J.R., Greve, D.N., Treadway, M.T., McGarvey, M., Quinn, B.T., Dusek, J.A., Benson, H., Rauch, S.L., Moore, C.I., & Fischl, B. (2005, November 28). Meditation experience is associated with increased cortical thickness. https://www.ncbi.nlm.nih.gov/pmc/articles/PMC1361002/

39 Moore, A. & Malinowski, P. (2009, January 31). Meditation, mindfulness and cognitive flexibility. https://www.sciencedirect.com/science/article/abs/pii/S1053810008001967

40 Black, D.S., O'Reilly, G.A., Olmstead, R., & et al. (2015, April). Mindfulness Meditation and Improvement in Sleep Quality and Daytime Impairment Among Older Adults With Sleep Disturbances: A Randomized Clinical Trial. https://jamanetwork.com/journals/jamaintern almedicine/fullarticle/2110998

41 Dean, J. (n.d.) 50 Per Cent More Motivation With This Way of Thinking About Rewards. http://www.spring.org.uk/2016/02/reward-versus-loss.php

42 University of Toronto. (2017, September 20). Motivation may be less limited than we think. ScienceDaily. Retrieved February 20, 2020 from www.sciencedaily.com/releases/2017/09/170920144701.htm

43 University of Toronto. (2017, September 20). Motivation may be less limited than we think. ScienceDaily. Retrieved February 20 2020 from www.sciencedaily.com/releases/2017/09/170920144701.htm

44 O'Neil, G. (n.d.) 5 Rules To Live By To Build Your Character During Chaos. http://hustlebranding.com/2013/08/07/5-rules-to-live-by-to-build-your-character-in-the-middle-of-chaos/

45 Barnosky, A.R., Hoddy, K.K., Unterman, T.G., & Varady, K.A. (2014, June 12). Intermittent fasting vs daily calorie restriction for type 2 diabetes prevention: a review of human findings. http://www.sciencedirect.com/science/article/pii/S193152441400200X

46 Ganesan, K., Habboush, Y., & Sultan, S. (2018, July 9). Intermittent Fasting: The Choice for a Healthier Lifestyle. https://www.ncbi.nlm.nih.gov/pmc/articles/PMC6128599/

47 Shevchuk, N.A. (2007, November 13). Adapted cold shower as a potential treatment for depression. http://www.sciencedirect.com/science/article/pii/S030698770700566X

48 Mooventhan, A. & Nivethitha, L. (2014, May). Scientific Evidence-Based Effects of

Hydrotherapy on Various Systems of the Body. https://www.ncbi.nlm.nih.gov/pmc/articles/PMC4049052/

49 Bleakley, C.M. & Davison, G.W. (2010, February). What is the biochemical and physiological rationale for using cold-water immersion in sports recovery? A systematic review. https://www.ncbi.nlm.nih.gov/pubmed/19945970

50 Shevchuk, N.A. & Radoja, S. (2007, November 13). Possible stimulation of anti-tumor immunity using repeated cold stress: a hypothesis. https://www.ncbi.nlm.nih.gov/pmc/articles/PMC2211456/

51 Rabenstein, T., Radaelli, F., & Zolk, O. (2012, October). Warm water infusion colonoscopy: a review and meta-analysis. https://www.ncbi.nlm.nih.gov/pubmed/22987214

52 Mayo Clinic Staff. (2018, November 21). Job burnout: How to spot it and take action. https://www.mayoclinic.org/healthy-

lifestyle/adult-health/in-depth/burnout/art-20046642

53 Maslach, C. & Leiter, M.P. (2016, June 5). Understanding the burnout experience: recent research and its implications for psychiatry. https://www.ncbi.nlm.nih.gov/pmc/articles/PMC4911781/

54 Shirom, A. & Melamed, S. (2006). A comparison of the construct validity of two burnout measures in two groups of professionals. https://psycnet.apa.org/record/2006-07100-003

55 Maslach, C. & Leiter, M.P. (2016, June 5). Understanding the burnout experience: recent research and its implications for psychiatry. https://www.ncbi.nlm.nih.gov/pmc/articles/PMC4911781/#wps20311-bib-0010

56 Heinemann, L.V. & Heinemann, T. (2017, January-March). Burnout Research: Emergence and Scientific Investigation of a Contested Diagnosis. https://journals.sagepub.com/doi/pdf/10.1177/2158244017697154

57 Roskam, I., Raes, M.E., & Mikolajczak, M. (2017, February 9). Exhausted Parents: Development and Preliminary Validation of the Parental Burnout Inventory. https://www.frontiersin.org/articles/10.3389/fpsyg.2017.00163/full

58 Kaschka, W.P., Korczak, D., & Broich, K. (2011, November 18). Burnout: a Fashionable Diagnosis. https://www.ncbi.nlm.nih.gov/pmc/articles/PMC3230825/

59 Bandura, A. (1977). Self-efficacy: Toward a unifying theory of behavioral change. https://psycnet.apa.org/record/1977-25733-001

60 Larner, A.J. (2016). A Dictionary of Neurological Signs. Springer. ISBN 978-3319298214. Archived from the original on 2016-12-24. Retrieved 2016-09-04.

61 Zeman, A., Dewar, M., & Della Sala, S. (2015, June 3). "Lives without imagery – Congenital aphantasia". https://www.pure.ed.ac.uk/ws/files/21561082/Sala_etal_C_2015_Lives_without_imagery.pdf

62 Childs, E. & de Wit, H. (2014, May 1). Regular exercise is associated with emotional resilience to acute stress in healthy adults. https://www.ncbi.nlm.nih.gov/pmc/articles/PMC4013452/

Self-Discipline Mastery

www.ingramcontent.com/pod-product-compliance
Lightning Source LLC
Chambersburg PA
CBHW051540020426
42333CB00016B/2016